Debunkum Beaver Pega How-to Guide

Installing and Testing AES

Copyright Notice

Disclaimer

Dedication & Acknowledgements

*First of all, I think we all need to thank
Alan Trefler, without him, there would not be the Pega
we are seeing today. It is also him, who kept Pega as a free company,
which was evident in the Reuters article on 'rather
eat sand than sell to other companies'.
Hopefully, Pega will continue
to be independent.*

*Special thanks to my dear wife
for the support provided for me to achieve
the CLSA certification, as well as the sacrificed family time
and encouragement she had provided me with to leverage on my academic
knowledge to contribute back to the community through this book.
Not to forget my boy, who volunteered to create a logo for
Debunkum Beaver, at the same time,
being my proof reader!*

*There were multiple great
SSAs/LSAs along my journey, who had
explained many important Pega concepts and guided
me in the past years. Their untiring explanations
and demonstrations are
greatly appreciated.*

*This book is a
dedication to all those who
would like to embark on the Pega Learning Journey.
With this, you now have one more
reliable resource.*

Contents

Who Is This Book For?

This Guide: **Debunkum Beaver Pega How-to Guide** is a series for everyone, people who are new to Pega as well as those who are experienced in Pega.

The prerequisite is just to have some basic understanding of Pega, preferably to have at least completed the Pega CSA training.

Being certified in Pega is not required, but a keen desire to learn Pega is a must!

Preface

Thanks for purchasing Debunkum Beaver Pega How-to Guide! In order to fully maximise the book, it is important to understand the purposes and positioning of this How-to series.

Why Create a Pega How-to Guide?
Strictly speaking, information on Pega "how-to" can be found in Pega Community, Pega Academy, as well as throughout the Internet.

Even if the information is not readily available, all that is needed is simply to create a new Pega Community post; and somehow, after some time, there would be people from the community, Pega GCS or even Pega Engineering, jumping in to provide the answer, so isn't such a how-to guide unnecessary?

Well, technically, you could argue it in that way. However, in any engagement, one of the most challenging things is "deadline". Often, a go-live date would be defined well before requirement specification is signed off.

Therefore, there is basically no time to search for information, wait for replies, or learn and explore how to implement certain features/requirements in an actual project scenario, at the time when it is required.

Apart from that, the replies are often not an end-to-end, step-by-step guide, complete with screenshots and do not include validation and testing steps. Thus, it would require prior Pega knowledge and additional effort to clarify, test and finally implement it.

To add on to the challenges, the profile of the team members often creates another dimension of issues. This problem has 2 extremities:

1) **<u>New Users of Pega:</u>** Those who are totally new to Pega
2) **<u>Senior and Experienced Pega SSA/LSA:</u>** Those who have many years of experiences, some even spanned across Pega V5.x and V6.x

For New Users of Pega, they do not know how to implement a lot of things in Pega, thus a lot of hand-holding and samples are required to guide them along and get them to be efficient.

There is technically not much issues with them, just the need to provide them with some relevant examples, or even implement one instance of the solution, explain to them how it works, and they would be able to get started and replicate the implementation across other parts of the application.

The downside is that a lot of time is required to create relevant samples and also to help them in debugging issues that may occur.

On the other hand, Senior and Experienced Pega SSAs/LSAs, although are self-starters and able to start implementation without much guidance, they introduced another kind of problem – their solutions to all problems are often "activities" and "agents"!!!

Any other issues that cropped up along the way, would often be yet another activity, custom Java codes or some HTML, JavaScripts; the worst that I have seen, was creating multiple Boolean variables to cater for various flows and decisions throughout the whole application for handle difference scenario and business changes!!!

With all those Boolean variables, in order to understand the whole logic (and ensure it is correct), you need to kept track of all the Boolean variables that are set/unset throughout all the activities, data transforms, flows, UIs, button clicked, etc.! Isn't that a BIG pain? How could the application ever be reliable?

Technically, they can implement the required features, but whatever they had touched, can no longer be easily modified by another SSA/LSA without the corresponding number of years of experience, not to mention about the underlying performance and maintenance issues that were introduced!

In view of all these challenges, Debunkum Beaver has decided to embark on this path: A How-to Guide for Pega.

For New Users of Pega, this series provide a step-by-step guide to implement any given feature; for Senior and Experienced Pega SSAs/LSAs, this guide shows the best practices and a standardised way of implementing the intended features, leveraging on the newer Pega capabilities to simplify the implementation, as much as possible.

With the Debunkum Beaver Pega How-to Guide series, you would have an arsenal of tools at your disposal. Whenever there is a new project, or a new feature required, all you have to do is just to pull out one of these guides. Cool right?

Can you visualise a situation, where all similar features have the same way of implementation, with the same sequence of steps and number of rules; and anyone who looked at the rules knew exactly how and why each rule was implemented as such; any deviations and bugs that were introduced due to carelessness would simply stand out by itself, easily identifiable and easy to fix, wouldn't this be a wonderful Pega World?

Well, that is the core objective of the **Debunkum Beaver Pega How-to Guide** series!

With the direction set, the next question is: "How Should I Categorise the Pega How-to Guide?"

How Should I Categorise the Pega How-to Guide?

Given that there are so many features, I couldn't just write <u>ONE book</u>, it would take ages, and by then, a new Pega version would be released!

Of course, I could potentially do a high-level grouping, e.g. *Pega Integration*, *Pega Reporting*, *Pega Case Management*, etc...

But there is one big problem...

Take *Pega Integration* as an example, there are so many types of integrations: SOAP, REST, OAuth2, etc. Does that mean that I should write all the integrations before publishing the *"Pega Integration"* book?

That would also take a long time, increase the overall price of the book and force readers to pay for things they don't need or are not interested in; worst, it would just end up as another version of Pega help file.

On top of that, if one of the integration methods changed, do I need to update the whole book as a new version?

Apart from the above issues, you may have realised another problem: I have not mentioned about another dimension of Integration: *Service Packages* vs *Service Connectors*!

So, should I have a book on *Pega Integration Service Connectors* and another on *Pega Integration Service Packages*? But I cannot separate them because I need to use the *Service Connectors* to invoke the *Service Packages* to test!

As you can see, things just get more and more messy...

I shared my problem with my boy, and asked him what books he enjoyed the most, and this is what he showed me - His private Mr Men Collection!

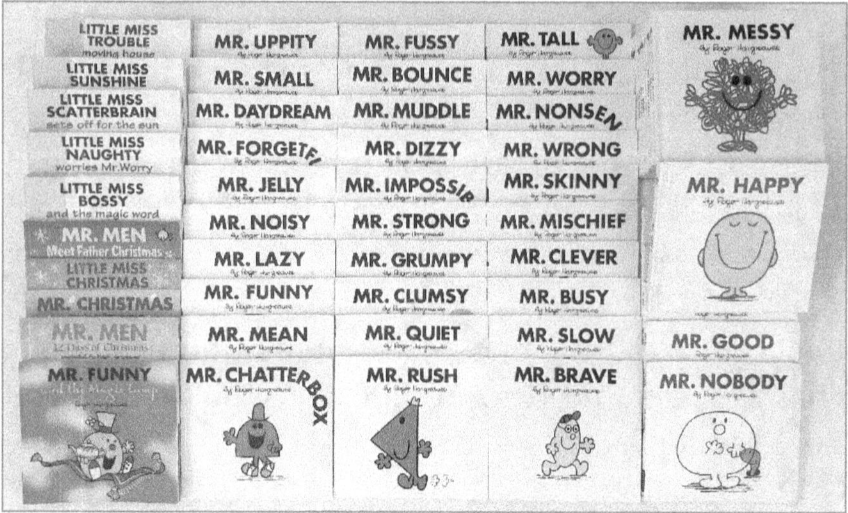

Figure 1: Mr Men Collection

He went on to explain how much he enjoyed the book. Although each single book is short, it is concise, and he can easily look for any Mr Men he wants; at the same time, priding himself as Mr Happy...

Well, although I feel Mr Messy is a better match for him , I agree on his concept: small little book that is concise, and easy to be used as a reference!

Yes! That is exactly how the Debunkum Beaver Pega How-to Guide would be released!

The next question is: How should I organise each Pega How-to Guide, so that it would achieve the core objective?

How Should I Organise Each Pega How-to Guide?

I want to have a how-to guide suitable for both beginners and experts, one that could be used as a quick reference, yet without the unnecessary theories and documentation.

Yes, this is really a tall order, but anything less than that would not serve the purpose and would just end up being another Pega Community post or simply an excerpt of the Pega help file!

It must be able to provide something like a 2-mins run-through to illustrate the purpose and concept, like the typical "Hello World!" of programming, yet able to be expanded further into more useful stuff!

So here, Debunkum Beaver Pega How-to Guide is born! It sets out to achieve the above by applying the following:

1) Quick explanation of the purpose of the feature
2) A quick implementation using the typical "Hello World" style, demonstrating the feature in the simplest form
3) Expansion of the example using various scenario and extension of the feature to cover related areas

In order to provide a quick explanation and make understanding of Pega concepts a breeze, at times, I might "state" that a given Pega feature is equivalent to something that is more commonly understood, followed by a series of scenario that further extend its capabilities and enable users to slowly appreciate the differences.

For example, I might start by stating: "Think of Pega Data classes as Database tables...", and then proceeded with some scenario on how to use Pega Data Classes to add, update and delete records, followed by other interesting features, that would extend it capability and moved beyond just database tables.

So, take note of this unique approach in the guide.

Versions of Pega How-To Guide

In order to launch the book fast and to keep cost down, as well as to contribute to the overall Pega community knowledge, the Pega How-to Guide will be released in 3 versions:

1) **Online Version:** This is a free version, published at DebunkumBeaver.com. Basically, selected chapters are published and contained all the information required to implement the intended feature. The details and quality of the instructions would often exceed those that are freely available on the Internet.

2) **How-to Version**: This version contains all the details steps, including complete screenshots on how to implement the intended feature. You can be sure that it would DEFINITELY work, because I would simplify the steps, and redo it from scratch. Anything lesser than that would not meet the earlier set out objectives, agree?

3) **Master Beaver Version**: This version contains everything of the How-to Version, with the inclusion of analysis and reasons for doing the

given steps, as well as special scenario and limitations of the feature.

Which Version Should I Get?

<u>Online Version</u>

If you are an experienced Pega architect and just need some pointers and have the time to investigate and try out the details, this version suits your needs.

By comparing this version with the How-to version, You will be able to better appreciate my purpose of creating the Pega How-to Guide series, as well as its value.

<u>How-to Version</u>

This version is for people who just want to implement the feature in the quickest possible way. This version takes the readers through a step-by-step procedure, with complete screenshots, thus suitable for new users of Pega, who wants to learn how to implement various features in Pega.

<u>Master Beaver Version</u>

If you are looking for more in-depth discussion, understand how and why the given feature was done in that way. This version is for you.

Most importantly, if you are considering taking Pega CLSA certification, it is always better to get the Master Beaver Version.

Author's Profile

The author is a Pega CLSA, certified in the new Pega CLSA Path (7.3/7.4). Academically, he has a master's degree and has experiences in teaching undergraduates pursuing master's and bachelor's degrees in World renowned universities.

Combining the above with his over 20 years of IT experiences in various MNCs, the author decided to write this series of Pega How-to Guide to help aspiring system architects to implement Pega in a faster, cleaner and more efficient way.

Why Not Do This At Pega Community?

This is an interesting option that I had considered before. However, there are a few stoppers:

Limited and Lack of Control

I hate the feeling of being restricted. I have many ideas, plans and ways of doing things, but when there are people or situations that restrict or delay me, I get very pissed off.

Lack of Details

Pega Community is good but more often than not, the replies are just one-liner, link to other articles, and a bunch of description and steps, which would not help if you do not have good Pega knowledge in the first place. Interestingly, if you had that, you wouldn't need to go there to search for answer in the first place!

Do take note that I am not saying that Pega Community does not provide good information or solutions, it is just that it was not meant to teach and guide you like what you were taught in your undergraduate studies.

I Want To Teach and Have Students Who Want to Learn

The platform today, and possibly many years into the future, focuses on the technicality of how to do a task, not about the purpose, or the thought process that led to the solution, which is a crucial skill you would want to acquire if you want to pass the exams.

I needed a platform to allow me to do that, but in Pega Community, people have a stronger tendency to listen only to those 'renowned professional', who sometimes went down the 'too technical' path.

Therefore, there is basically no avenue that I could share the detailed and vast knowledge that I have.

Since I am an author, have the academic background, as well as a Pega CLSA, it makes perfect sense for me to do it through publication, thus, the birth of this book.

I want to teach, and if you want to learn, then welcome to the mind-blowing world of Debunkum Beaver!

Introduction

In this chapter, we will touch on the scope of this guide and some quick description of AES (Autonomic Event Services).

You can contact Pega for the AES Application Bundle as well as the list of hotfixes (as mentioned below).

This guide demonstrates how to install and ensure that your AES is working. The information is based on the following URL:

https://community.pega.com/knowledgebase/installing-pega-autonomic-event-services-73

Why Create This "Installing and Testing AES" Pega How-to Guide?

Firstly, if you follow the instruction closely, it will not work.

Secondly, if you have noticed, _**ALL**_ Pega help files and many articles are without the necessary images. Even if there are, many are often zoomed in so much that you would not be able to appreciate the context of the step without launching Pega Designer Studio.

Interestingly, I had suggested for screenshots in the help files, etc. However, the general thinking is that having screenshots would tend to create more work and make the instructions outdate faster.

Although I don't agree with the viewpoint, there is nothing I can do. Therefore, I decided to go ahead and create it according to the way I want it to be, thus, the birth of this book: "Debunkum Beaver Pega How-to Guide: Installing and Testing AES"!

For this guide, I had gone through the process of installing and testing AES, and presented all the relevant screenshots to you. At the same time, highlighting specific issues along with the instructions.

This will make it easier for anyone who is interested to install and test AES, accomplish the task in a much faster and efficient way!

About This Pega How-to Guide: Installing and Testing AES

This Pega How-to Guide: Installing and Testing AES contains information on installing and testing AES.

The first question I have about AES is: It seems that Pega is moving to cloud, and Pega also have PDC (Predictive Diagnostic Cloud), why would customer be installing AES?

Well, there are many customers still doing that. I recently did one for a customer, and their reason for doing this is simple: Who would want to send their diagnostics information over the cloud to Pega?

Bear in mind that from most customers' perspective, diagnostics information is sensitive.

If you have ever done application hardening before, you would come across a clause that states:

"NO ERROR MESSAGES and NO DIAGNOSTICS INFORMATION should appear on the screen"!

If you take a look at the OWASP™ Foundation, you will also see the point being reiterated:

Is the Application Vulnerable?

The application might be vulnerable if the application is:

- Missing appropriate security hardening across any part of the application stack, or improperly configured permissions on cloud services.
- Unnecessary features are enabled or installed (e.g. unnecessary ports, services, pages, accounts, or privileges).
- Default accounts and their passwords still enabled and unchanged.
- Error handling reveals stack traces or other overly informative error messages to users.
- For upgraded systems, latest security features are disabled or not configured securely.
- The security settings in the application servers, application frameworks (e.g. Struts, Spring, ASP.NET), libraries, databases, etc. not set to secure values.
- The server does not send security headers or directives or they are not set to secure values.
- The software is out of date or vulnerable (see **A9:2017-Using Components with Known Vulnerabilities**).

Without a concerted, repeatable application security configuration process, systems are at a higher risk.

Figure 2: OWASP™ Foundation Application Vulnerability Checklist

Therefore, if error messages and diagnostics information are not allowed to be shown on the screen, how could you expect customer to send that information over the cloud to a 3rd party site that is managed by another entity?

Anyway, that is beyond the scope of this book. I just want Pega to really think about this question and focus back on AES!

Of course, if expert monitoring and analysis could be bundled into the PDC, then it could potentially add some values to use PDC. That is: if you leverage on PDC, periodic advice and consultancy on your application tuning is included as part of the package.

Well, that is just my 2-cents worth. I shall focus back on the scope of this book instead.

Autonomic Event Services (AES) in a Nutshell

Pega Autonomic Event Services (AES) is an application that monitors the performance status of Pega Platform systems, installed on a stand-alone Pega Platform server.

In a nutshell, the core features of AES that I like are:
- Aggregation of error messages, their frequencies as well as prioritisation of their severity

- Scorecards for critical functions of Pega
- Notifications and emails for subscribed reports/scorecard

Without AES, there is basically no elegant ways of monitoring the performance of Pega platform, the next recourse would be to periodically look at log files or use log file monitoring tools, painful, right?

This document is based on the following:
- AES version 7.3
- Pega version 7.4 for AES server and the monitored system

Some of the information of this book is taken from:
https://community.pega.com/knowledgebase/pega-autonomic-event-services-hotfixes

Sadly, if you look at the above URLs and other related ones, you will see many of those having such top banner:

(i) This content has been archived and is no longer being maintained.

Figure 3: Content No Longer Being Maintained

Again, I sincerely hope Pega is in the process of revamping the information, *NOT* sunsetting AES for PDC.

Review the AES Hotfixes

As with all software, there is a list of pre-installation tasks to be performed. For installation of AES, we have the application bundle and a list of hotfixes.

According to the reference link earlier, you should import the AES Application Bundle before applying the hotfixes, as shown below.

Import hotfixes in the following order:

- Apply Pega Platform™ hotfixes immediately after a Pega Platform installation or upgrade.
- Apply Pega Autonomic Event Services hotfixes right after you complete the application bundle import.
- Apply monitored systems hotfixes right after you configure a system for monitoring with Pega Autonomic Event Services.

Figure 4: Import AES Application Bundle Before Hotfixes

It is assumed that you had already applied the relevant hotfixes for the Pega Platform before importing the AES Application Bundle. If you are not sure what are the list of Pega Platform hotfixes to apply, contact Pega Support, they will provide you with the list for your installation.

The list of AES hotfixes given in the URL above are listed below:

Hotfix number	Available since	Observed behavior
HFix-39121	December 6, 2017	*The perfdatamode property in the cluster record is reset, although a monitored Pega Platform instance is configured to use push mode.*

Hotfix number	Available since	Observed behavior
HFix-39225	December 6, 2017	Managers cannot restrict system visibility by using the Manage Operator Systems flow.
HFix-39044	December 6, 2017	When a user views a rule instance cache, an error in an activity causes a misleading error message.
HFix-39086	December 6, 2017	In Internet Explorer 11, Total Alerts by Node, Alerts by Category, and Exceptions by PCF reports might be incorrectly displayed.
HFix-39267	December 6, 2017	On the Agents tab and the Requestors tab, for a cluster with multiple nodes, Pega Autonomic Event Services displays data for one node only.
HFix-44436	July 3, 2018	The AES 7.3 user interface is not rendered correctly when running on Pega Platform 7.4.
HFix-46747	September 27, 2018	The nightly purge process deletes entries only from the PegaAES-Work-Exception and PegaAES-Work-Action class tables. As a result, unneeded entries in the PEGAAM_ACTION_INDEX table cause performance issues.
HFix-46796	October 4, 2018	For a system with multiple active nodes, on the Enterprise landing page Summary tab, Pega Autonomic Event Services displays data for one node only.
HFix-47290	October 4, 2018	For a system with multiple nodes, on the Enterprise landing page Requestorstab, Pega Autonomic Event Services displays duplicates of requestors.
HFix-47600	October 4, 2018	Data about newly added nodes is not available, because the D_ReachableNodes data page is not refreshed.
HFix-47601	October 12, 2018	In the Agents tab, the Enabled column displays information incorrectly.
HFix-48448	November 2, 2018	The ExecuteGetActivityData activity always returns the same message, regardless of the result of the node reachability test.
HFix-48132	November 5, 2018	In the Recent Alerts report, clicking an alert does not open the corresponding case.
HFix-49975	January 14, 2019	In the Action Item Reports section, the Exception Items - By Exception Class and Alerts - By Category reports run for all systems by default, because they do not use the current system as a filter condition.
HFix-50178	January 31, 2019	Data that is displayed on the Dashboard is two days old.

Yes, it is a very long list, again, I have no idea why Pega did not package all the above as 1 service pack... Such that there is only a need to install once, not 15 times...

Import AES Application Bundle

After you have login to Pega, such as using the default user name `administrator@pega.com` with the default password of `install`, click *Designer Studio > Application > Distribution > Import* as shown below:

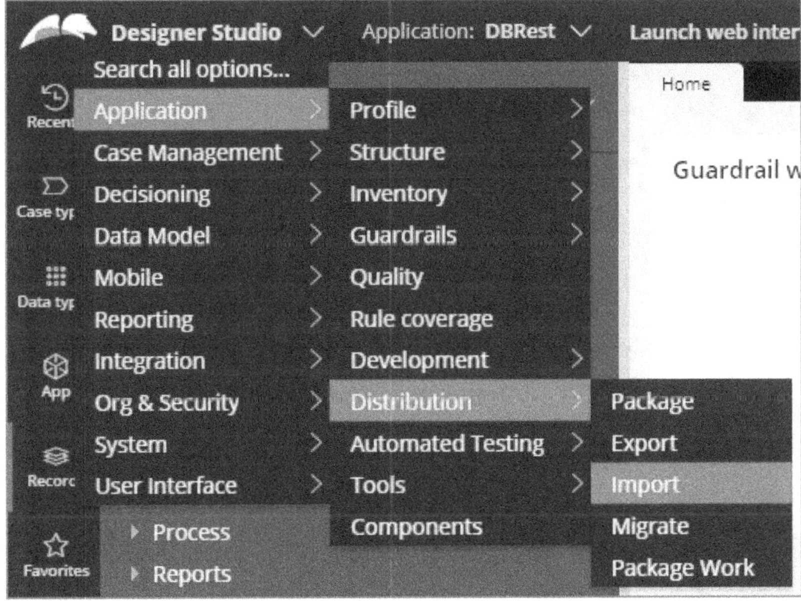

Figure 5: Accessing the Import Menu

In the following screen, select "Local file", then click on the "Choose File" button to select the application build, which should have the name:

AES_07_30_01.jar. After that, click the "Next" button.

Figure 6: Selecting the AES Application Bundle

The file information will be displayed, similar to the following. Click "Next" to continue.

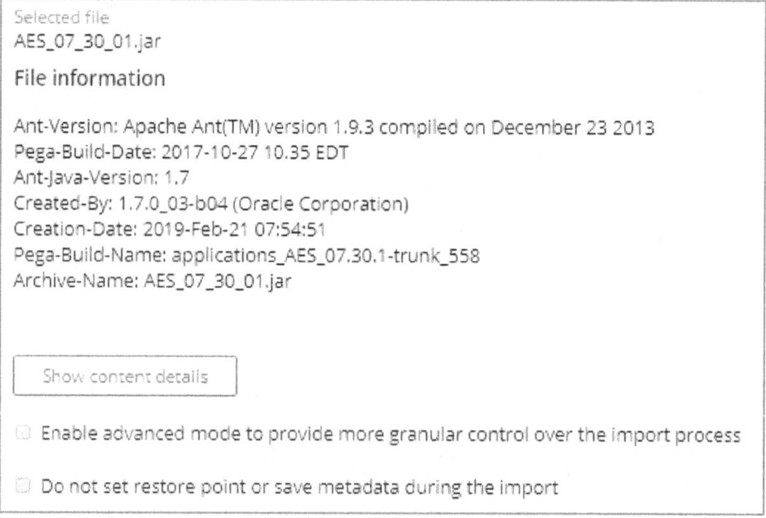

Figure 7: File Information for AES_07_30_01.jar

You will now see this message. Make sure that the "Total errors" is showing "0".

Import complete to database from the file lib

100.00%

Time left: 0 seconds

Total records: 1   Records moved: **1**   Records skipped: 0   Total errors: 0

Import included code archives, restart PRPC to activate.

Figure 8: Summary Message

It is assumed that you had already applied the relevant hotfixes for the Pega Platform before importing the AES Application Bundle.

Your screens and filenames might not be exactly the same as the above.

Continue the wizard, taking most of the defaults, and you should see a list of screens similar to the following:

⇒ Schema

The bundle requires changes to the database schema.

In order for this application to work correctly, these schema changes must be applied.

◉ Automatic: Schema changes will be applied automatically using the database user defined in the database configuration.
○ Manual: The database schema changes are applied manually by using the button below to download the SQL DDL script.

If you wish to execute the schema changes manually you should apply them before you continue with the wizard.

Download the SQL DDL, execute the schema and continue the wizard or restart.

To view SQL DDL double click on a table or view.

|◄ ◄ Page 1   of 2 ► ►|

Class	Table	Has DB Schema Changes
History-PegaAES-Data-SystemMetrics	pr_History_PegaAES_Data_System	Yes
History-PegaAES-Work-Action	pc_history_work	No
History-PegaAES-Work-Exception	pc_history_work	No
Index-PegaAES-Data-DailyMetric	pegaam_dailymetrics_index	Yes
Index-PegaAESAppClusName	pegaam_action_index	Yes
PegaAES-Data-Alert	pegaam_alert	Yes
PegaAES-Data-Cluster	pegaam_cluster_data	Yes
PegaAES-Data-Conf-GradeThreshold	pegaam_conf	Yes
PegaAES-Data-CriticalEvent	pegaam_crit_event	Yes
PegaAES-Data-DailyMetrics	pegaam_dailymetrics	Yes
PegaAES-Data-EmailRecipient	pegaam_email_recipient	Yes
PegaAES-Data-Exception	pegaam_exception	Yes
PegaAES-Data-GCEvent	pegaam_gc_event	Yes
PegaAES-Data-Guardrail	pegaam_guardrail	Yes
PegaAES-Data-Index	pegaam_index	Yes
PegaAES-Data-Indicator	pegaam_indicator	Yes
PegaAES-Data-IndicatorChange	pegaam_ind_change	Yes
PegaAES-Data-LogUsage	pegaam_perf_stats	Yes
PegaAES-Data-MonitoringStats-Cluster	pegaam_monitoringstatscluster	Yes
PegaAES-Data-MonitoringStats-Node	pegaam_monitoringstatsnode	Yes

Selected	Class	View	Has DB Schema Changes
No views to import			

View/Download SQL DDL

Figure 9: Pega Schema Changes Screens Page 1/2

⇒ Schema

The bundle requires changes to the database schema.

In order for this application to work correctly, these schema changes must be applied.

◉ Automatic: Schema changes will be applied automatically using the database user defined in the database configuration.
◯ Manual: The database schema changes are applied manually by using the button below to download the SQL DDL script.

If you wish to execute the schema changes manually you should apply them before you continue with the wizard.

Download the SQL DDL, execute the schema and continue the wizard or restart.

To view SQL DDL double click on a table or view.

⏮ ◀ Page 2 of 2 ▶ ⏭

Class	Table	Has DB Schema Changes
PegaAES-Data-NodeHealth	pegaam_node_health	Yes
PegaAES-Data-NodeStats	pegaam_node_stats	Yes
PegaAES-Data-Nodes	pegaam_cluster_data	Yes
PegaAES-Data-RSSnapshot	pegaam_rssnapshot	Yes
PegaAES-Data-RSSnapshotChange	pegaam_rssnapshot_chg	Yes
PegaAES-Data-RemoteReport	pegaam_remote_report_data	Yes
PegaAES-Data-SQLStates	pegaam_sql_states	Yes
PegaAES-Data-SystemLogStats	pegaam_stdlog_stats	Yes
PegaAES-Data-SystemMetrics	pegaam_system_metrics	Yes
PegaAES-Data-TopOffenders	pegaam_topoffenders	Yes
PegaAES-Internal-ProcessingInfo	pegaam_processing_info	Yes
PegaAES-Work-Action	pegaam_action_work	Yes
PegaAES-Work-Exception	pegaam_exception_work	Yes
PegaAESRemote-Interface-IndexData	pr_index_info	Yes

Selected	Class	View	Has DB Schema Changes
No views to import			

[View/Download SQL DDL]

Figure 10: Pega Schema Changes Screens Page 2/2

One interesting thing about Pega is that it is able to compare your target system with your import package, then automatically generate a list of SQL DDL to synchronise the changes.

This capability supports moving between different OS, web servers, and most importantly, databases.

This is also the reason why you should avoid DB specific codes, such as those RDB stuff.

If you are interested, you can click on the "View/download SQL DDL" to download the generated DDL.

Another usage of this generated DDL is that in some customer environment, you may not be able to run SQL directly on their systems, especially for UAT and PROD environments.

This downloaded SQL can then be passed over to the customer DBA to execute; once the SQL is executed, you can then proceed with other steps.

Other subsequent screens are shown below:

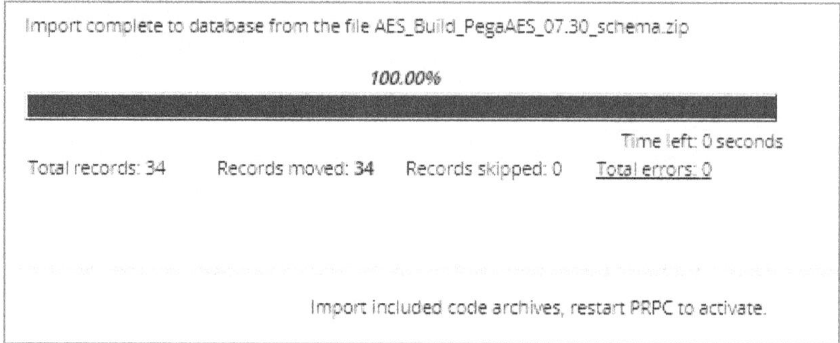

Figure 11: Schema Import Completed

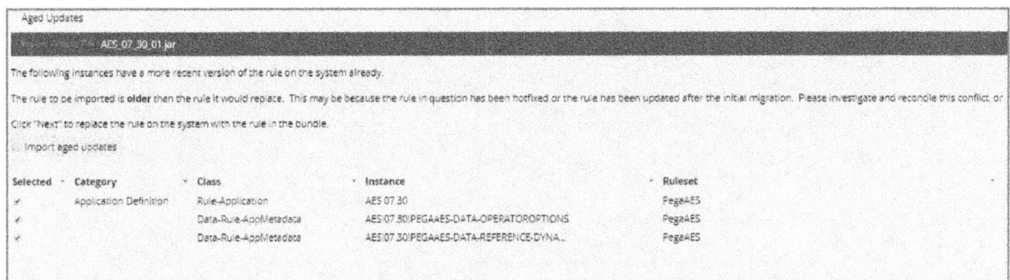

Figure 12: Avoid Importing Aged Updates

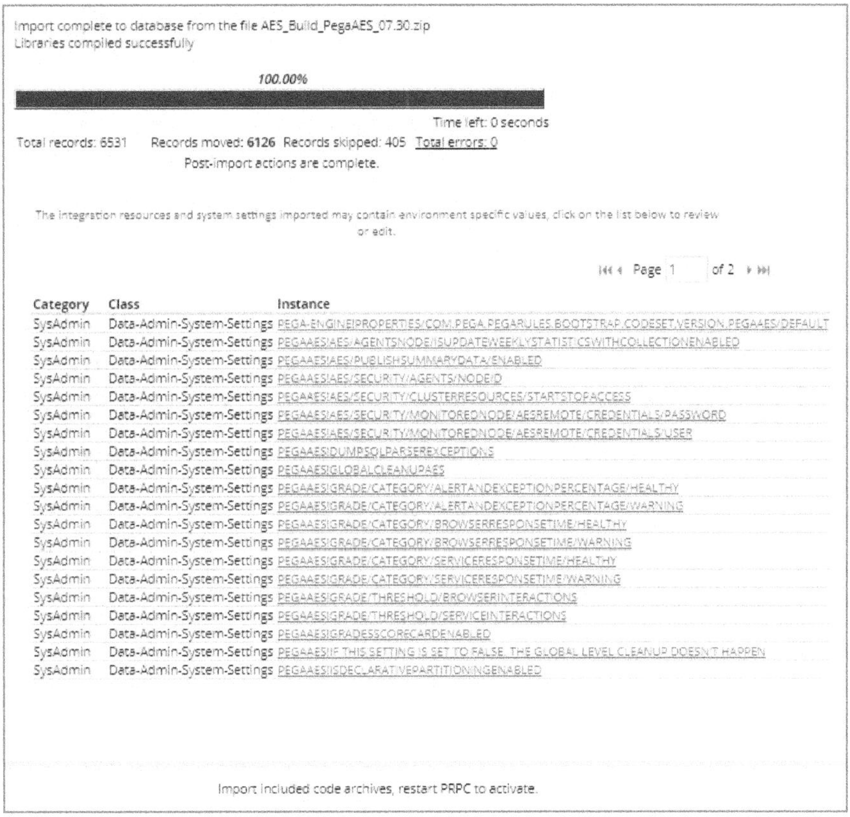

Import complete to database from the file AES_Build_PegaAES_07.30.zip
Libraries compiled successfully

100.00%

Time left: 0 seconds
Total records: 6531   Records moved: **6126** Records skipped: 405 Total errors: 0
Post-import actions are complete.

The integration resources and system settings imported may contain environment specific values, click on the list below to review or edit.

|◄◄ ◄ Page 1   of 2 ► ►►|

Category	Class	Instance
SysAdmin	Data-Admin-System-Settings	PEGA-ENGINE!PROPERTIES/COM.PEGA.PEGARULES.BOOTSTRAP.CODESET.VERSION.PEGAAES/DEFAULT
SysAdmin	Data-Admin-System-Settings	PEGAAES!AES/AGENTSNODE/ISUPDATEWEEKLYSTATISTICSWITHCOLLECTIONENABLED
SysAdmin	Data-Admin-System-Settings	PEGAAES!AES/PUBLISHSUMMARYDATA/ENABLED
SysAdmin	Data-Admin-System-Settings	PEGAAES!AES/SECURITY/AGENTS/NODEID
SysAdmin	Data-Admin-System-Settings	PEGAAES!AES/SECURITY/CLUSTERRESOURCES/STARTSTOPACCESS
SysAdmin	Data-Admin-System-Settings	PEGAAES!AES/SECURITY/MONITOREDNODE/AESREMOTE/CREDENTIALS/PASSWORD
SysAdmin	Data-Admin-System-Settings	PEGAAES!AES/SECURITY/MONITOREDNODE/AESREMOTE/CREDENTIALS/USER
SysAdmin	Data-Admin-System-Settings	PEGAAES!DUMPSQLPARSEREXCEPTIONS
SysAdmin	Data-Admin-System-Settings	PEGAAES!GLOBALCLEANUPAES
SysAdmin	Data-Admin-System-Settings	PEGAAES!GRADE/CATEGORY/ALERTANDEXCEPTIONPERCENTAGE/HEALTHY
SysAdmin	Data-Admin-System-Settings	PEGAAES!GRADE/CATEGORY/ALERTANDEXCEPTIONPERCENTAGE/WARNING
SysAdmin	Data-Admin-System-Settings	PEGAAES!GRADE/CATEGORY/BROWSERRESPONSETIME/HEALTHY
SysAdmin	Data-Admin-System-Settings	PEGAAES!GRADE/CATEGORY/BROWSERRESPONSETIME/WARNING
SysAdmin	Data-Admin-System-Settings	PEGAAES!GRADE/CATEGORY/SERVICERESPONSETIME/HEALTHY
SysAdmin	Data-Admin-System-Settings	PEGAAES!GRADE/CATEGORY/SERVICERESPONSETIME/WARNING
SysAdmin	Data-Admin-System-Settings	PEGAAES!GRADE/THRESHOLD/BROWSERINTERACTIONS
SysAdmin	Data-Admin-System-Settings	PEGAAES!GRADE/THRESHOLD/SERVICEINTERACTIONS
SysAdmin	Data-Admin-System-Settings	PEGAAES!GRADESSCORECARDENABLED
SysAdmin	Data-Admin-System-Settings	PEGAAES!IF THIS SETTING IS SET TO FALSE, THE GLOBAL LEVEL CLEANUP DOESN'T HAPPEN
SysAdmin	Data-Admin-System-Settings	PEGAAES!ISDECLARATIVEPARTITIONINGENABLED

Import included code archives, restart PRPC to activate.

Figure 13: Post-Import Actions Completed

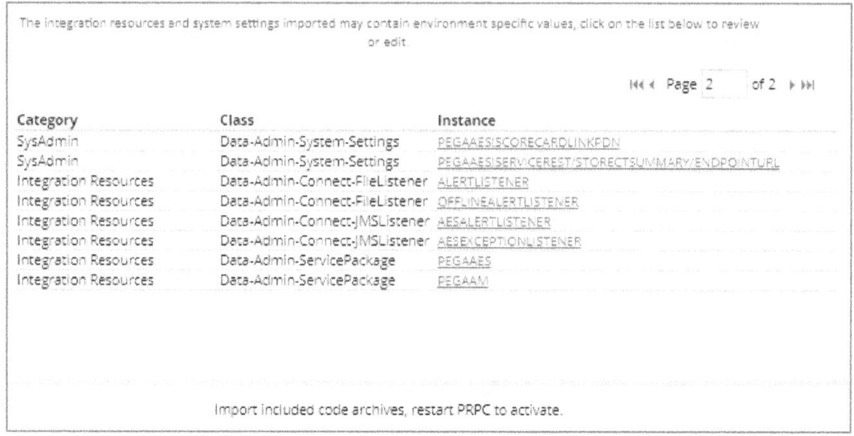

Figure 14: Other Relevant Screens in the AES Application Bundle Import

There is really no need to go into every single detail of the above, most of the time you can just take the defaults. There are 2 things that you need to be aware:

1) Make sure in all the "complete" screen, the "total errors" is always 0. The "Total records" and "Records moved" could be different due to your system already having the rules or that yours is a newer version.

2) For the *"Import aged updates"* checkbox in *"Figure 12: Avoid Importing Aged Updates"* above, you should keep it untick, unless you are intentionally trying to override your existing rules.

If you use a Microsoft SQL Server, ask the database administrator to run the following database statement:
EXEC sp_rename
'<var><Pega_schema></var>.pegaam_action_work.clusterName',
'ClusterName', 'COLUMN';

Where <Pega_schema> is the name of the Data schema.

I did not run the above as I am not using SQL Server. If you encounter any issues, always check with Pega Support.

After you have done the above, restart the Pega instance that you have just installed the AES. If you are using VM, you can simply just restart the whole VM.

Installing the Hotfixes

There is no specific instruction on the order of installation; in general, I just installed it from the top to the bottom of the given table above.

For this section, I will just share with you the screenshots that I had for each of the hotfixes.

Please bear in mind that you MUST always obtain the hotfixes from Pega Support and use the version that you are given.

If there is any deviation, you should follow those that are given by Pega Support.

 *There is a very high chance that your "Records moved" and "Records skipped" numbers in the hotfixes are different from mine. This is perfectly normal since your based system might already have some hotfixes that I don't. However, you need to ensure that the "Total errors" is 0 in all your hotfixes completion screens.*

To launch the hotfix installation for AES, click: *Designer Studio > Application > Distribution > Import* as shown below:

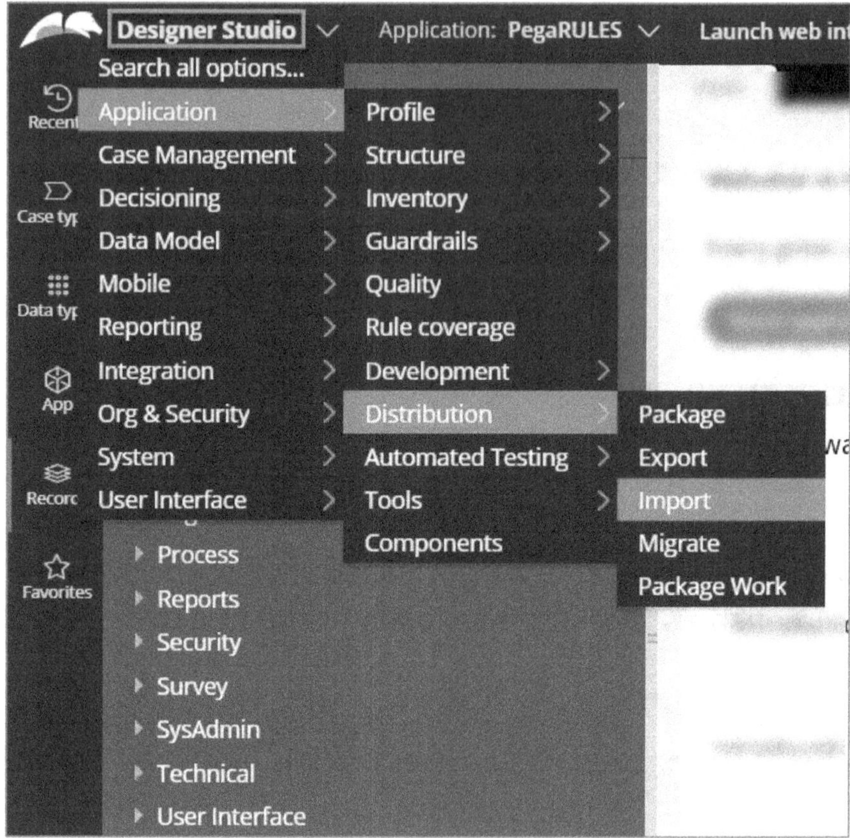

Figure 15: Menu Navigation for AES Hotfixes Installation

The above procedure needs to be performed for each of the hotfixes.

HFix-39121

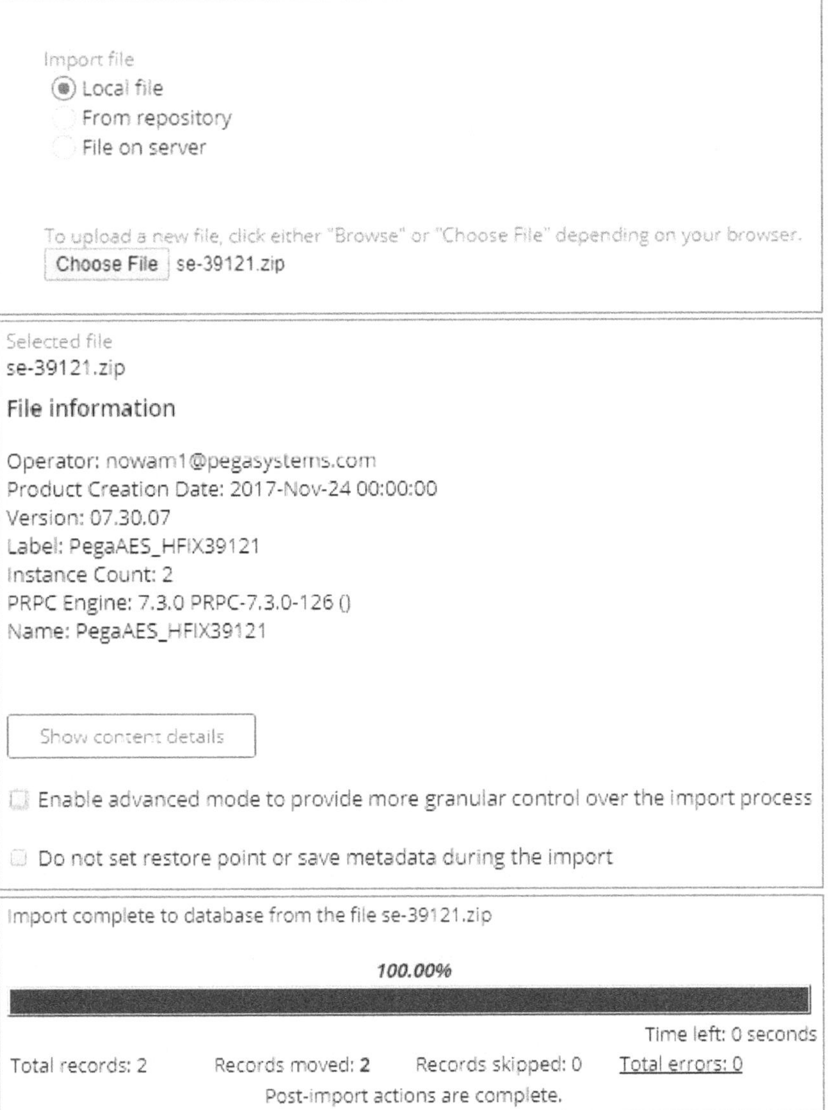

Figure 16: Screenshots for HFix-39121

HFix-39225

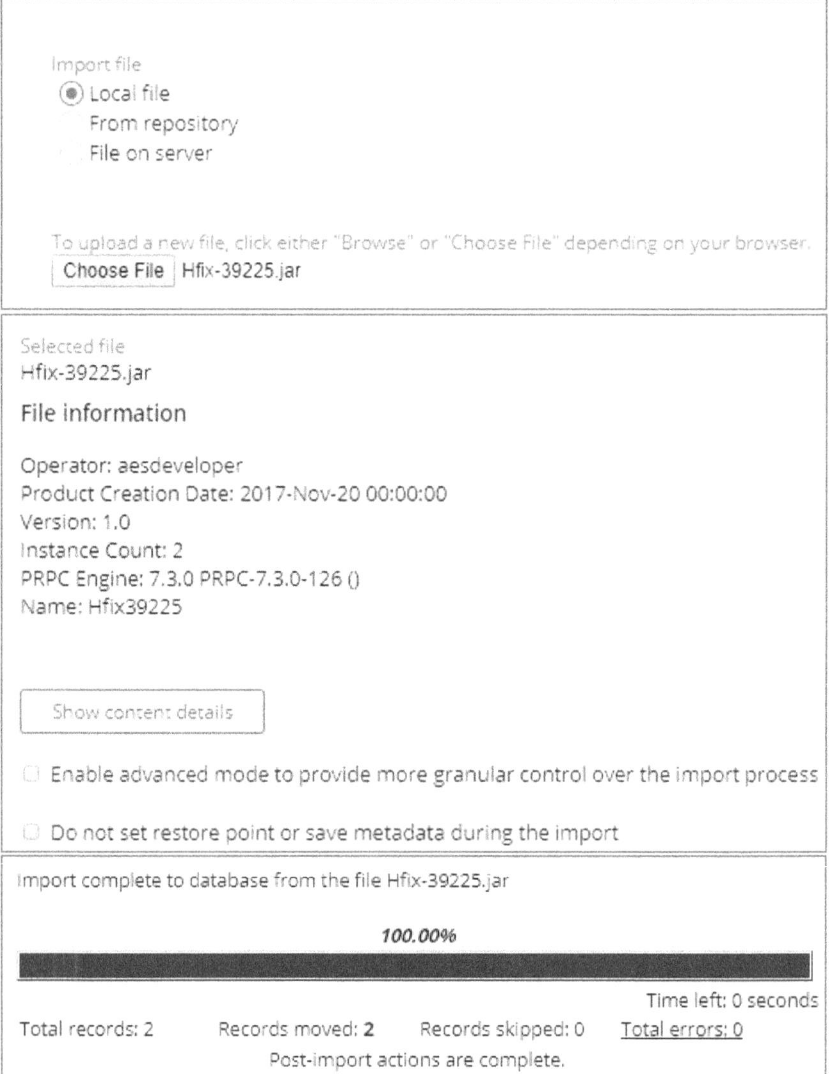

Figure 17: Screenshots for HFix-39225

HFix-39044

Import file
- ◉ Local file
- ○ From repository
- ○ File on server

To upload a new file, click either "Browse" or "Choose File" depending on your browser.

| Choose File | HFIX-39044.zip

Selected file
HFIX-39044.zip

File information

Operator: werda@pegasystems.com
Product Creation Date: 2017-Nov-15 00:00:00
Version: 07.30.04
Instance Count: 2
PRPC Engine: 7.3.0 PRPC-7.3.0-126 ()
Name: PegaAESHFIXSE39044

Show content details

☐ Enable advanced mode to provide more granular control over the import process

☐ Do not set restore point or save metadata during the import

---

Import complete to database from the file HFIX-39044.zip

100.00%

Time left: 0 seconds

Total records: 2   Records moved: **2**   Records skipped: 0   Total errors: 0

Post-import actions are complete.

Figure 18: Screenshots for HFix-39044

HFix-39086

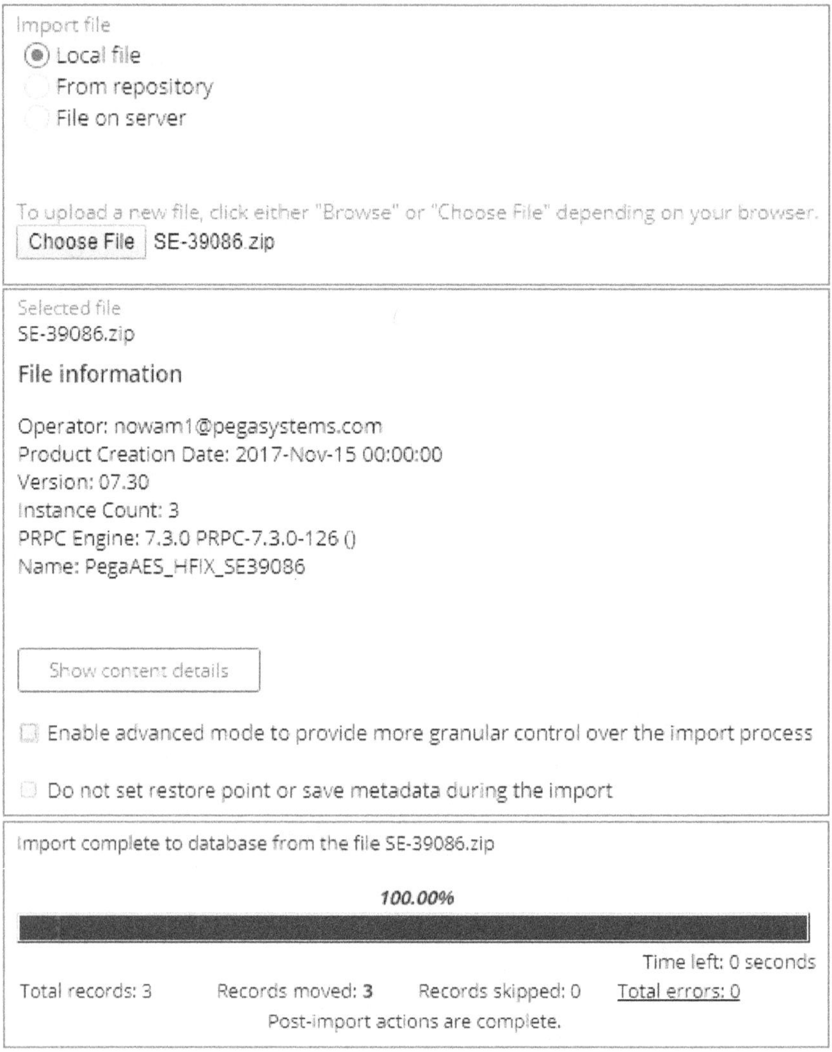

Import file
- ( ) Local file
- ( ) From repository
- ( ) File on server

To upload a new file, click either "Browse" or "Choose File" depending on your browser.

Choose File   SE-39086.zip

Selected file
SE-39086.zip

File information

Operator: nowam1@pegasystems.com
Product Creation Date: 2017-Nov-15 00:00:00
Version: 07.30
Instance Count: 3
PRPC Engine: 7.3.0 PRPC-7.3.0-126 ()
Name: PegaAES_HFIX_SE39086

Show content details

☐ Enable advanced mode to provide more granular control over the import process

☐ Do not set restore point or save metadata during the import

Import complete to database from the file SE-39086.zip

100.00%

Time left: 0 seconds

Total records: 3   Records moved: **3**   Records skipped: 0   Total errors: 0

Post-import actions are complete.

Figure 19: Screenshots for HFix-39086

HFix-39267

Import file
- Local file
- From repository
- File on server

To upload a new file, click either "Browse" or "Choose File" depending on your browser.

Choose File | Hfix-39267.zip

Selected file
Hfix-39267.zip

File information

Operator: werda@pegasystems.com
Product Creation Date: 2017-Dec-01 00:00:00
Version: Hfix-39267
Instance Count: 4
PRPC Engine: 7.3.0 PRPC-7.3.0-126 ()
Name: Hfix39267

Show content details

- Enable advanced mode to provide more granular control over the import process

- Do not set restore point or save metadata during the import

Import complete to database from the file Hfix-39267.zip

100.00%

Time left: 0 seconds

Total records: 4   Records moved: **4**   Records skipped: 0   Total errors: 0

Post-import actions are complete.

Figure 20: Screenshots for HFix-39267

HFix-44436

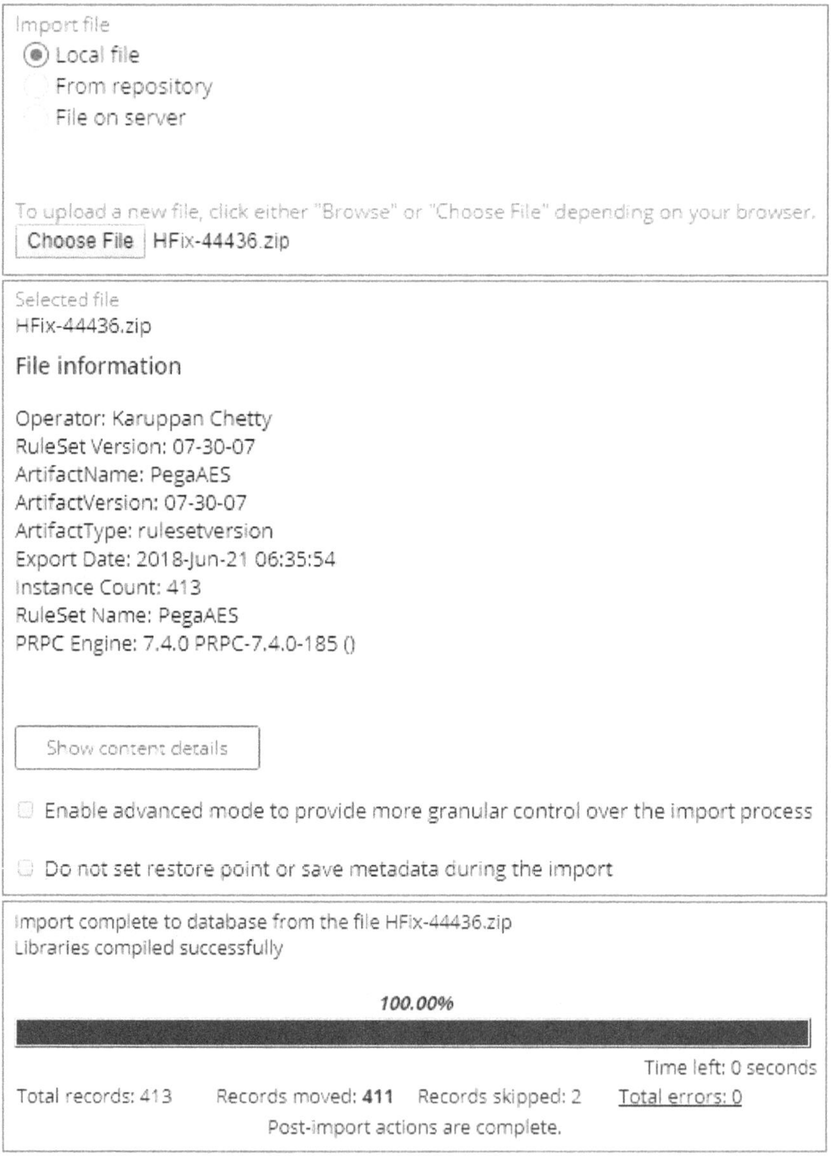

Import file
- ⦿ Local file
- ○ From repository
- ○ File on server

To upload a new file, click either "Browse" or "Choose File" depending on your browser.
| Choose File | HFix-44436.zip

Selected file
HFix-44436.zip

File information

Operator: Karuppan Chetty
RuleSet Version: 07-30-07
ArtifactName: PegaAES
ArtifactVersion: 07-30-07
ArtifactType: rulesetversion
Export Date: 2018-Jun-21 06:35:54
Instance Count: 413
RuleSet Name: PegaAES
PRPC Engine: 7.4.0 PRPC-7.4.0-185 ()

| Show content details |

☐ Enable advanced mode to provide more granular control over the import process

☐ Do not set restore point or save metadata during the import

Import complete to database from the file HFix-44436.zip
Libraries compiled successfully

100.00%

Time left: 0 seconds

Total records: 413   Records moved: **411**   Records skipped: 2   Total errors: 0
Post-import actions are complete.

Figure 21: Screenshots for HFix-44436

HFix-46747

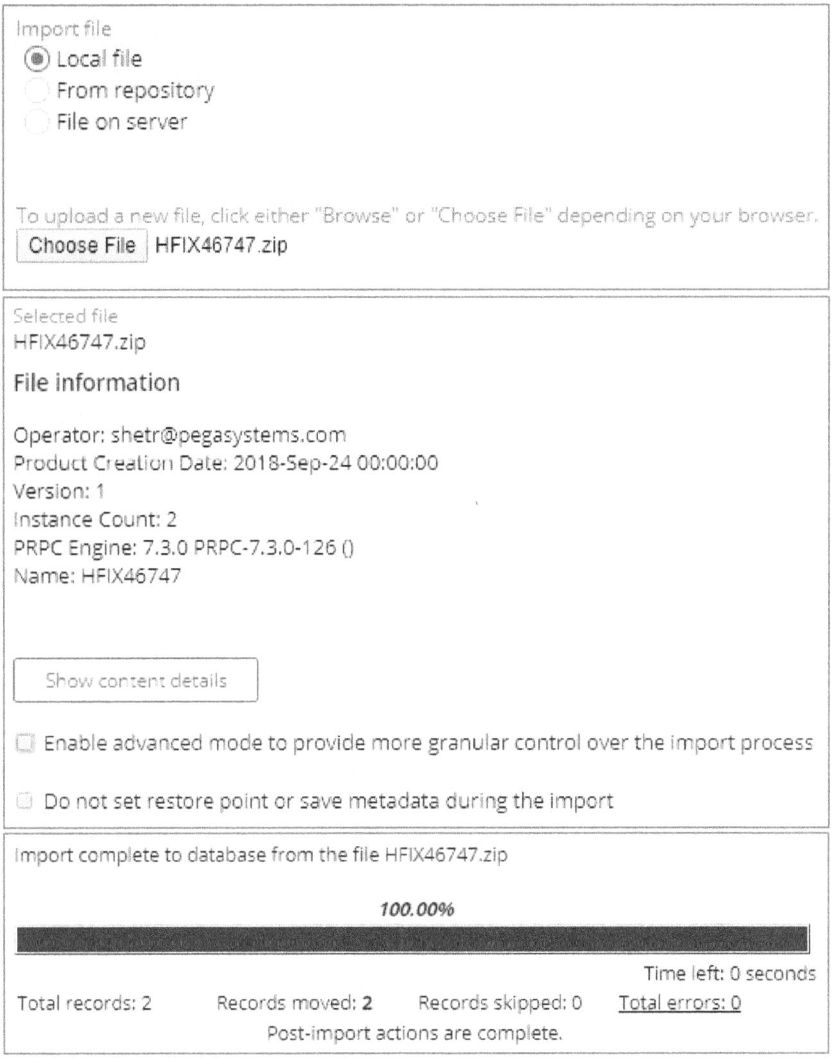

Import file
- ◉ Local file
- ○ From repository
- ○ File on server

To upload a new file, click either "Browse" or "Choose File" depending on your browser.

Choose File | HFIX46747.zip

Selected file
HFIX46747.zip

File information

Operator: shetr@pegasystems.com
Product Creation Date: 2018-Sep-24 00:00:00
Version: 1
Instance Count: 2
PRPC Engine: 7.3.0 PRPC-7.3.0-126 ()
Name: HFIX46747

Show content details

☐ Enable advanced mode to provide more granular control over the import process

☐ Do not set restore point or save metadata during the import

---

Import complete to database from the file HFIX46747.zip

100.00%

Time left: 0 seconds

Total records: 2   Records moved: **2**   Records skipped: 0   Total errors: 0

Post-import actions are complete.

Figure 22: Screenshots for HFix-46747

HFix-46796

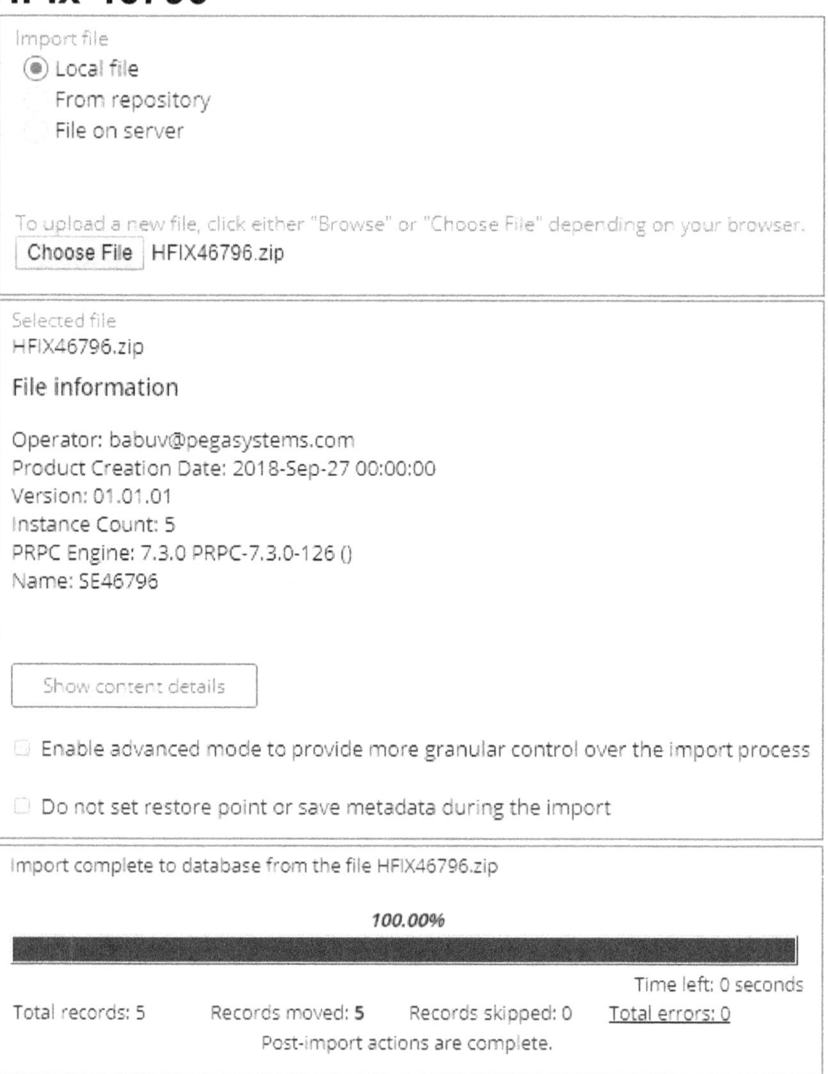

Figure 23: Screenshots for HFix-46796

HFix-47290

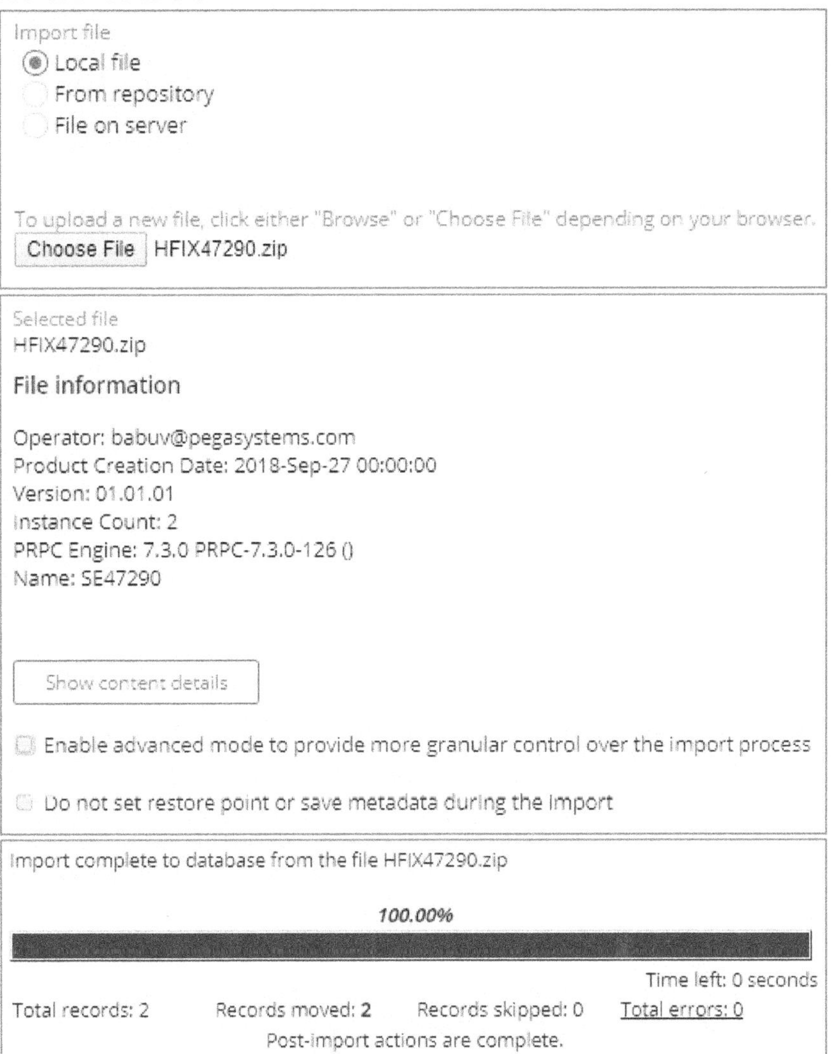

Figure 24: Screenshots for HFix-47290

HFix-47600

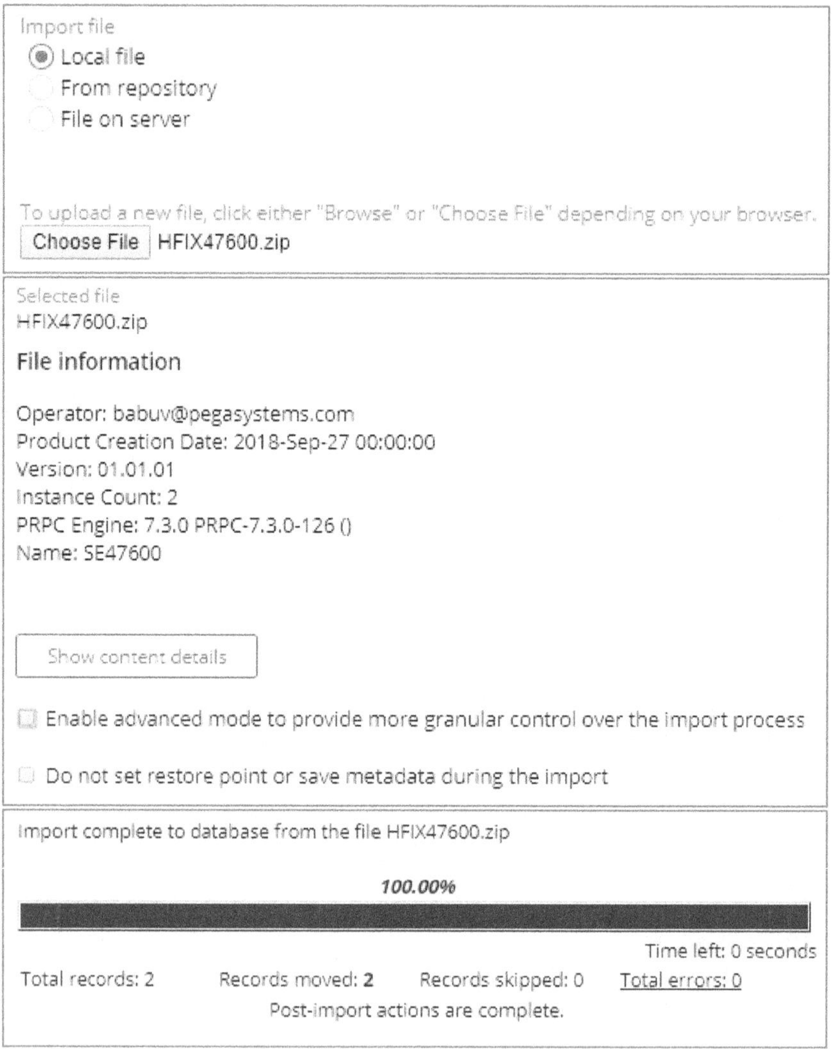

Import file
- ⦿ Local file
- ○ From repository
- ○ File on server

To upload a new file, click either "Browse" or "Choose File" depending on your browser.

Choose File | HFIX47600.zip

Selected file
HFIX47600.zip

File information

Operator: babuv@pegasystems.com
Product Creation Date: 2018-Sep-27 00:00:00
Version: 01.01.01
Instance Count: 2
PRPC Engine: 7.3.0 PRPC-7.3.0-126 ()
Name: SE47600

Show content details

☐ Enable advanced mode to provide more granular control over the import process

☐ Do not set restore point or save metadata during the import

---

Import complete to database from the file HFIX47600.zip

100.00%

Time left: 0 seconds

Total records: 2   Records moved: **2**   Records skipped: 0   Total errors: 0

Post-import actions are complete.

Figure 25: Screenshots for HFix-47600

HFix-47601

Import file
- ● Local file
- ○ From repository
- ○ File on server

To upload a new file, click either "Browse" or "Choose File" depending on your browser.

Choose File | HFIX47601.zip

Selected file
HFIX47601.zip

File information

Operator: aesdeveloper
ArtifactName: PegaAES073015
Name: PegaAES073015
ArtifactVersion: 01
Product Creation Date: 2018-Oct-09 00:00:00
Version: 01
ArtifactType: product
Export Date: 2018-Oct-10 00:07:59
Instance Count: 3
PRPC Engine: 7.4.0 PRPC-7.4.0-185 ()

Show content details

☐ Enable advanced mode to provide more granular control over the import process

☐ Do not set restore point or save metadata during the import

Import complete to database from the file HFIX47601.zip

100.00%

Time left: 0 seconds

Total records: 3   Records moved: **3**   Records skipped: 0   Total errors: 0

Post-import actions are complete.

Figure 26: Screenshots for HFix-47601

HFix-48448

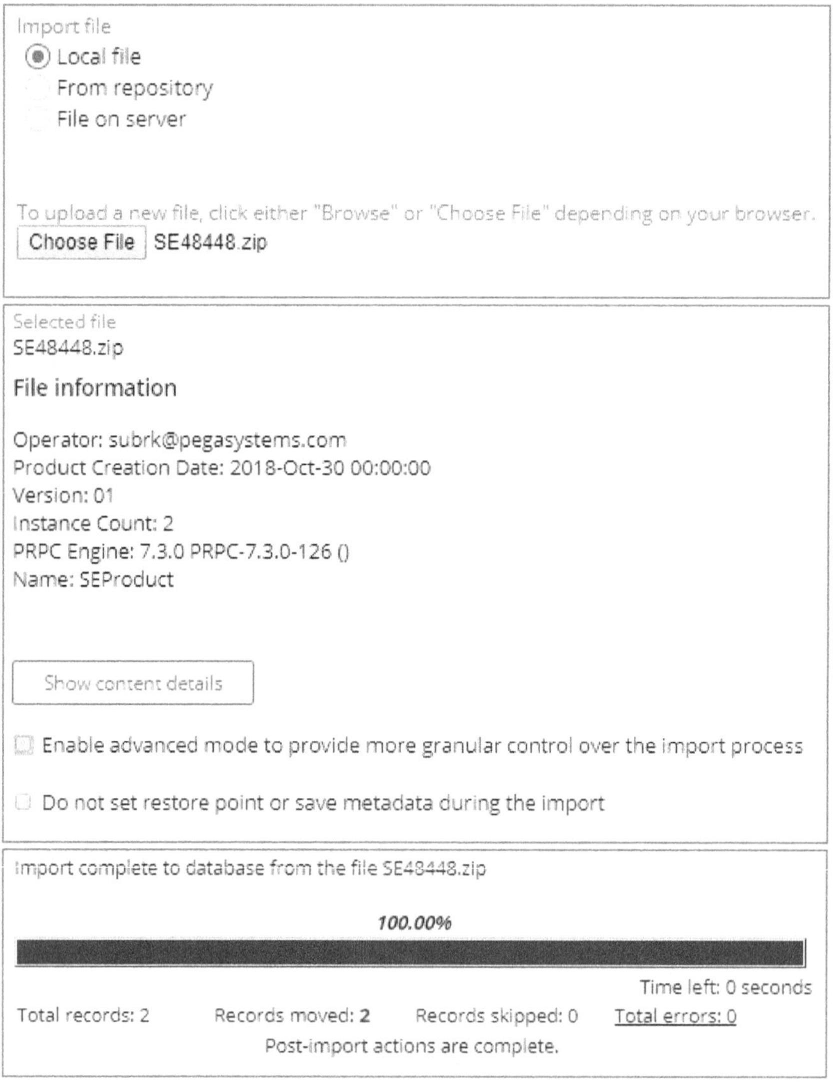

Import file
- (●) Local file
- ( ) From repository
- ( ) File on server

To upload a new file, click either "Browse" or "Choose File" depending on your browser.

[Choose File] SE48448.zip

Selected file
SE48448.zip

File information

Operator: subrk@pegasystems.com
Product Creation Date: 2018-Oct-30 00:00:00
Version: 01
Instance Count: 2
PRPC Engine: 7.3.0 PRPC-7.3.0-126 ()
Name: SEProduct

[Show content details]

☐ Enable advanced mode to provide more granular control over the import process

☐ Do not set restore point or save metadata during the import

Import complete to database from the file SE48448.zip

100.00%

Time left: 0 seconds

Total records: 2   Records moved: **2**   Records skipped: 0   Total errors: 0

Post-import actions are complete.

Figure 27: Screenshots for HFix-48448

HFix-48132

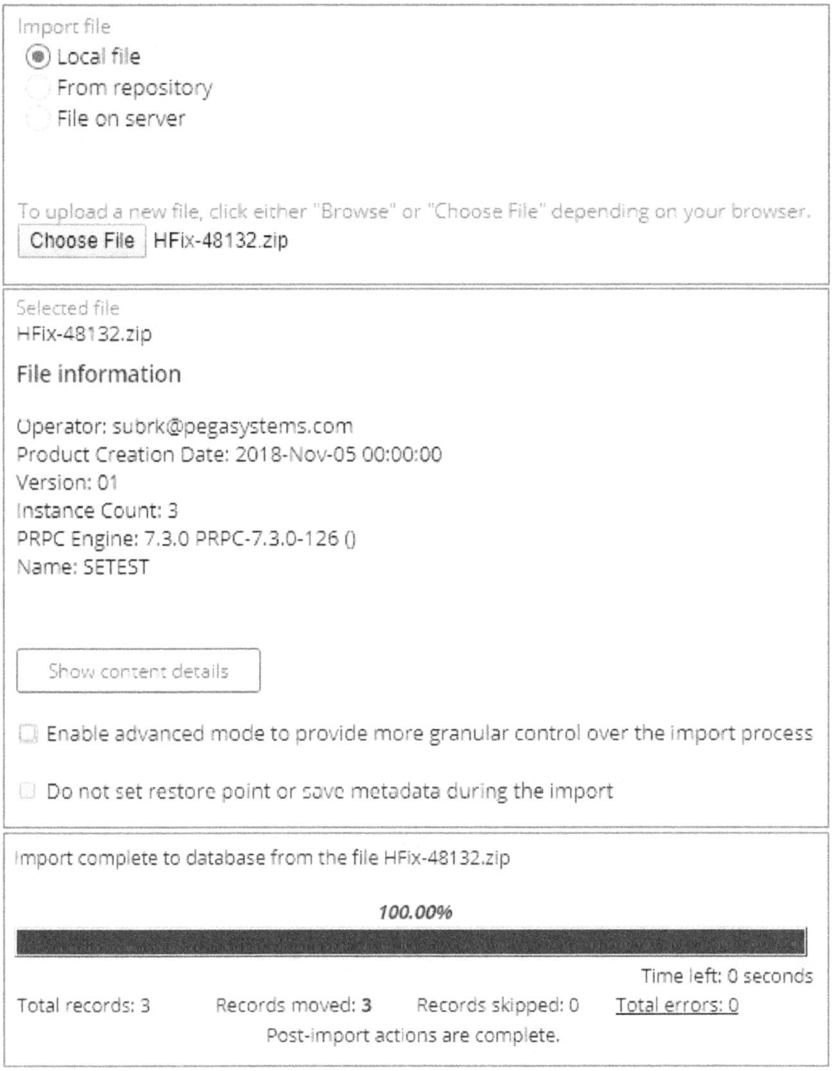

Import file
- (•) Local file
- ( ) From repository
- ( ) File on server

To upload a new file, click either "Browse" or "Choose File" depending on your browser.

| Choose File | HFix-48132.zip

Selected file
HFix-48132.zip

File information

Operator: subrk@pegasystems.com
Product Creation Date: 2018-Nov-05 00:00:00
Version: 01
Instance Count: 3
PRPC Engine: 7.3.0 PRPC-7.3.0-126 ()
Name: SETEST

[Show content details]

☐ Enable advanced mode to provide more granular control over the import process

☐ Do not set restore point or save metadata during the import

Import complete to database from the file HFix-48132.zip

100.00%

Time left: 0 seconds

Total records: 3   Records moved: **3**   Records skipped: 0   Total errors: 0

Post-import actions are complete.

Figure 28: Screenshots for HFix-48132

HFix-49975

Import file
- ◉ Local file
- ○ From repository
- ○ File on server

To upload a new file, click either "Browse" or "Choose File" depending on your browser.

Choose File | HFix-49975.zip

Selected file
HFix-49975.zip

File information

Operator: babuv@pegasystems.com
Product Creation Date: 2018-Dec-07 00:00:00
Version: 01.01.01
Label: PegaAES-Patch-07-30-17
Instance Count: 3
PRPC Engine: 7.3.0 PRPC-7.3.0-126 ()
Name: PegaAESPatch073018

Show content details

☐ Enable advanced mode to provide more granular control over the import process

☐ Do not set restore point or save metadata during the import

Import complete to database from the file HFix-49975.zip

100.00%

Time left: 0 seconds

Total records: 3　　Records moved: **3**　　Records skipped: 0　　Total errors: 0
Post-import actions are complete.

Figure 29: Screenshots for HFix-49975

HFix-50178

Import file
- ◉ Local file
- ○ From repository
- ○ File on server

To upload a new file, click either "Browse" or "Choose File" depending on your browser.

[Choose File] HFIX-50178.zip

Selected file
HFIX-50178.zip

File information

Operator: patna@pegasystems.com
Product Creation Date: 2019-Jan-23 00:00:00
Version: 01.01.01
Label: HFIX50178
Instance Count: 8
PRPC Engine: 7.3.0 PRPC-7.3.0-126 ()
Name: HFix50178

[Show content details]

☐ Enable advanced mode to provide more granular control over the import process

☐ Do not set restore point or save metadata during the import

---

Import complete to database from the file HFIX-50178.zip

100.00%

Time left: 0 seconds

Total records: 8   Records moved: **8**   Records skipped: 0   Total errors: 0

Post-import actions are complete.

Figure 30: Screenshots for HFix-50178

Remember Pega Hotfix Manager?

If you recall, Pega has a Hotfix Manager, accessed through the following:

Designer Studio > System > Release > Hotfix Manager:

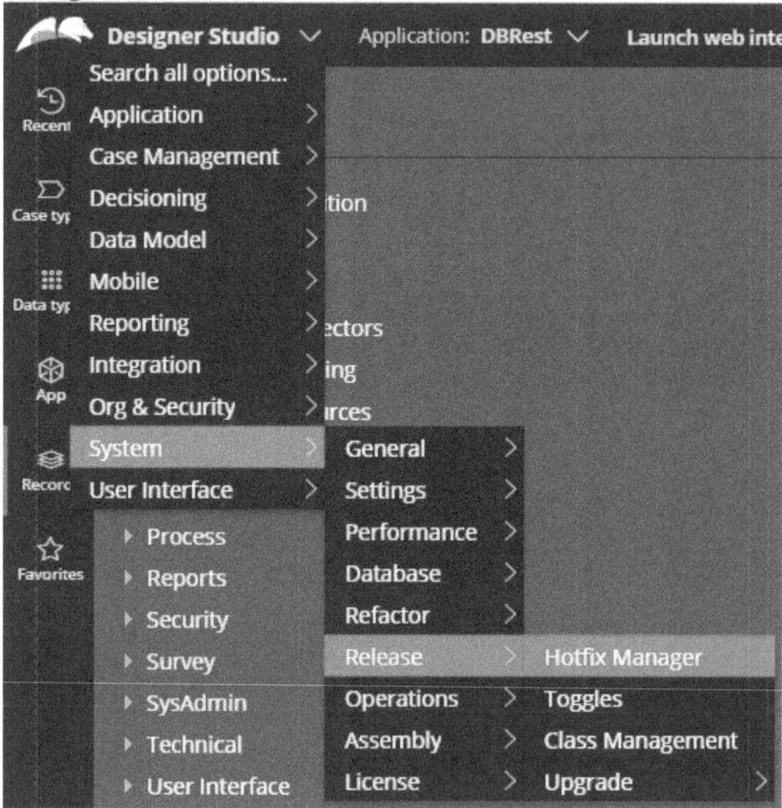

Figure 31: Accessing Pega Hotfix Manager

Once clicked, you will be presented with the following:

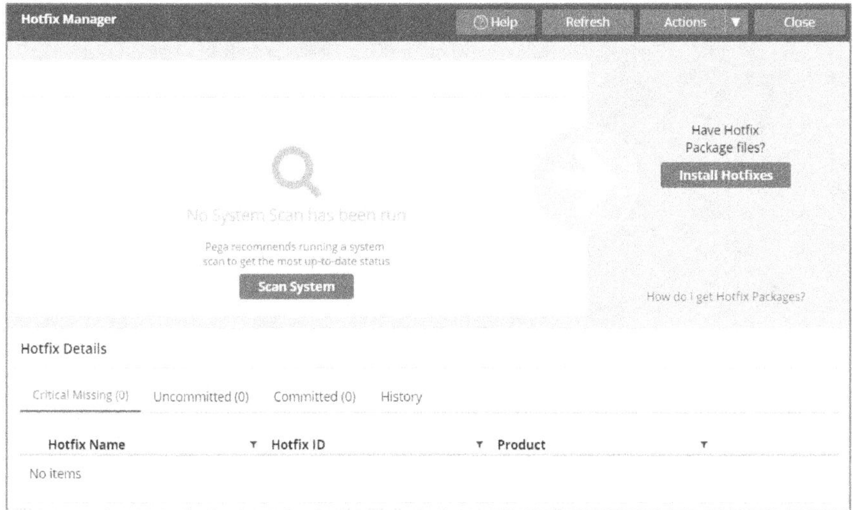

Figure 32: Pega Hotfix Manager

The beauty of Hotfix Manager is that you could apply the fix, test it out and do a rollback later if it doesn't work! So why didn't we use this?

Well, it turns out that you don't really have a choice. What I observed is that hotfixes that are meant for Hotfix Manager has the format `DL_zzzz.zip`, where `zzzz` is a series of digits representing the hotfix package number.

Other type of hotfixes would generally require using the "Application Import" functionality as what we did above.

Generally, if in doubt, always refer to the readme file in the package to decide how to apply it, or log a support ticket with Pega to clarify.

Verifying AES Installation

The next step is to validate your AES installation. To do that, login with the user name `aesdeveloper`. The default password is `password`.

Unable to Login as "aesdeveloper"?

If you are using Pega 7.4 onwards, you will realise that you are not able to login using the `aesdeveloper` because Pega had added a new security layer, where all newly imported users are disabled by default.

To resolve this, you need to login as another administrator, e.g. `administrator@pega.com` with the default password of `install`. Followed by searching for the `aesdeveloper`.

The easiest way to search for an operator is to enter it into the search box (located at the top right of the Designer Studio), followed by clicking on the search icon (🔍) as shown below.

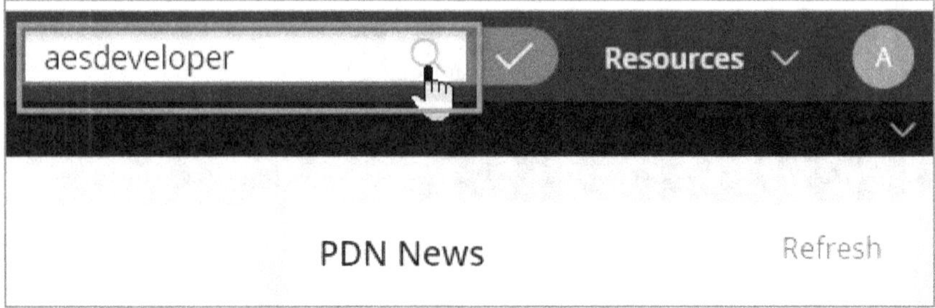

Figure 33: Searching for Rules in Pega

The following shows the list of rules matching your search.

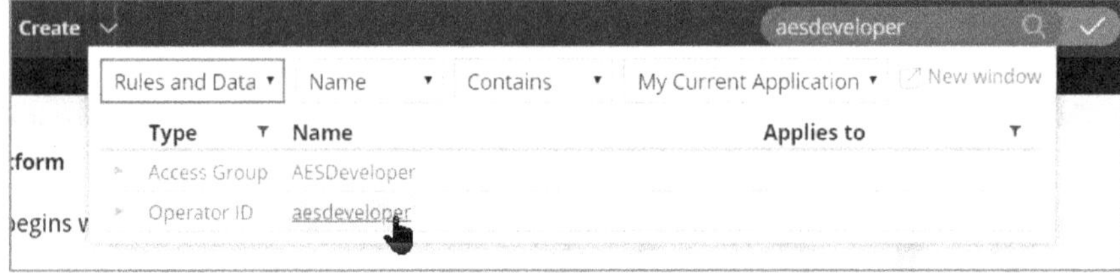

Figure 34: Search Results for aesdeveloper

Since we are looking for Operator ID, click on the *"aesdeveloper"* of the "Operator ID" row, which will open the *aesdeveloper* operator rule.

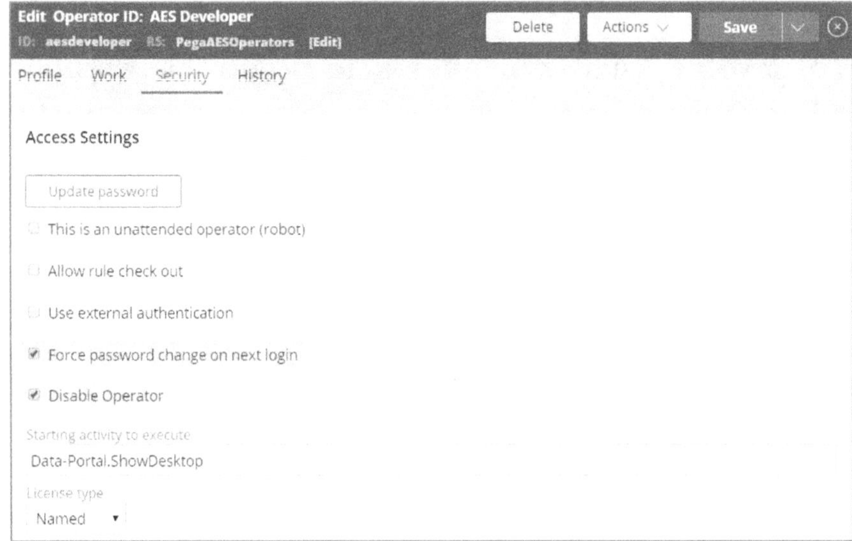

Figure 35: Initial AES Developer Operator Set As Disabled

You will notice that the *Force password change on next login* and *disable Operator* are both ticked.

To make things simple (for development and learning purposes), you should untick these. However, if you were to untick both at the same time and save, you would get the following error message:

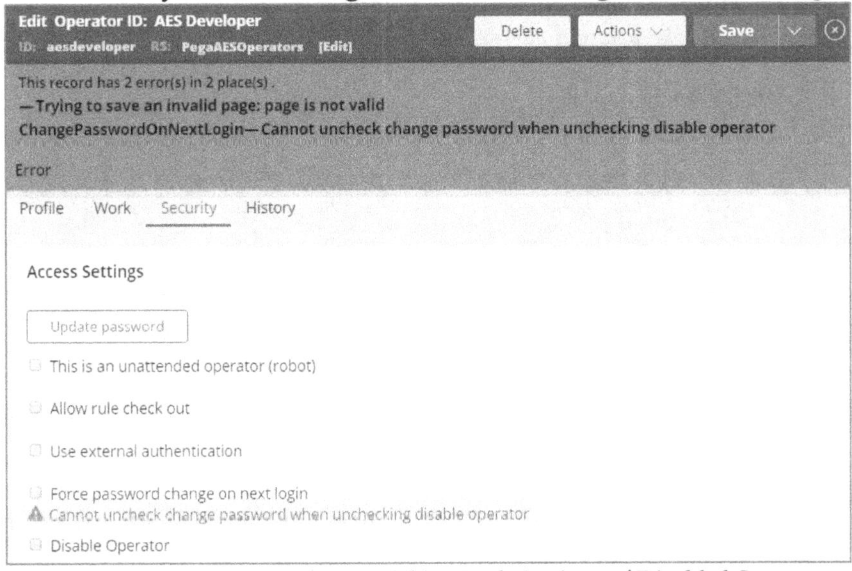

Figure 36: Error Message When Unticking Both Options of Disabled Operator

To resolve this, tick only the *Force password change on next login,* and click the "Save" button to save it. Once saved, untick the *Force password change on next login,* and click the "Save" button again.

Close this rule, and logout of Designer Studio, then login as *aesdeveloper* again, with the default password of *password* (if you have not changed it) to continue the next section.

Verifying the Installation of Rulesets

After you have login as `aesdeveloper`, (depending on your versions and settings, you might be asked to change the password, if so, follow the instruction accordingly).

> *If you had unticked the "Force password change on next login", you will not be prompted to change the password. For development and training systems, you might just want to use the default password for this user (i.e. password) or change to the generic "rules" password. No matter what you decide, always remember the password.*

> *If you had forgotten any operator password, just follow the instruction in the earlier section: "Unable to Login as aesdeveloper" and click on the "Update password" button shown there. This only works for Pega managed authentication, other forms of authentication are managed externally and is beyond the scope of this guide.*
>
> *Note once again, this is meant for training purposes.*

After you have successfully login, you should notice that the application is "AES":

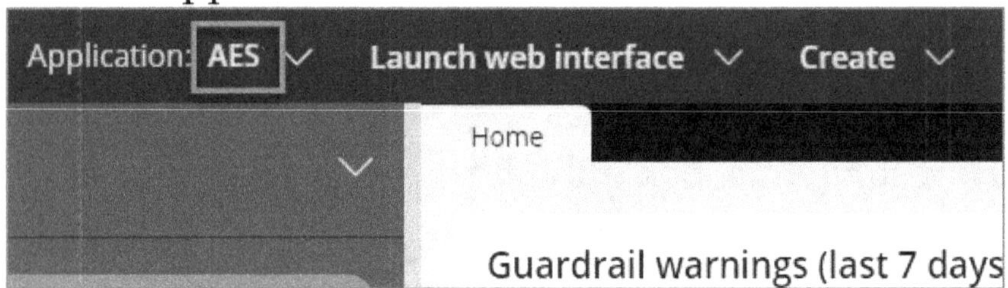

Figure 37: Default AES Application for AES Developer

In Designer Studio, click: ***Designer Studio > Application > Structure > RuleSet Stack***, as shown below

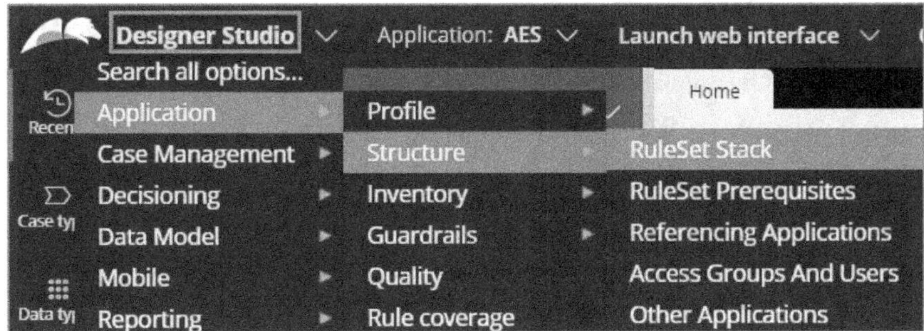

Figure 38: Opening the RuleSet Stack of AES Application

In the opened form, verify that the following ruleset versions are listed:

- PegaAESCriteria:01-01-01
- PegaAES:07-30-01

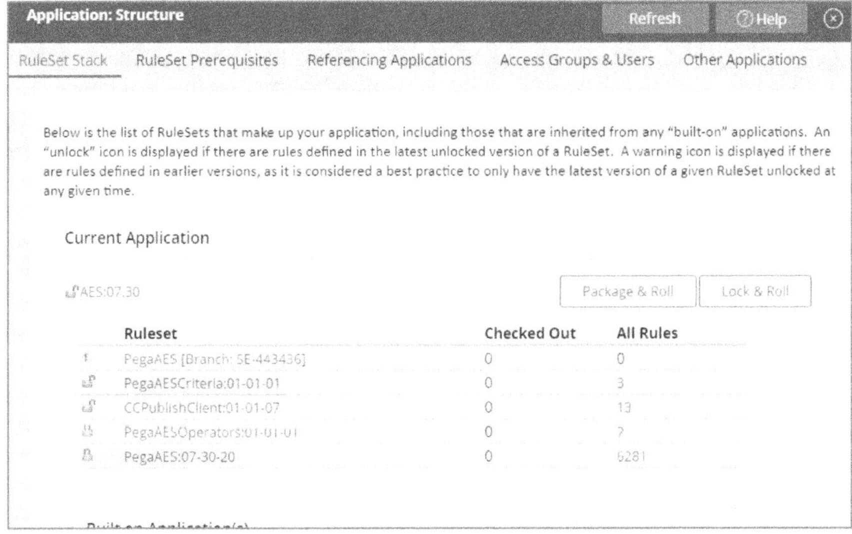

Figure 39: PegaAESCriteria and PegaAES Rulesets

The instruction in the Pega documentation stated PegaAES:07-30-01", but mine is "PegaAES:07-30-20". That does not matter since mine is of a newer version.

If your system does not contain the latest rulesets, the installation was not completed successfully. You need to contact Pega support for assistance.

Testing the AES Install

While still in Designer Studio, launch either the AES User Portal or the AES Manager Portal as shown below:

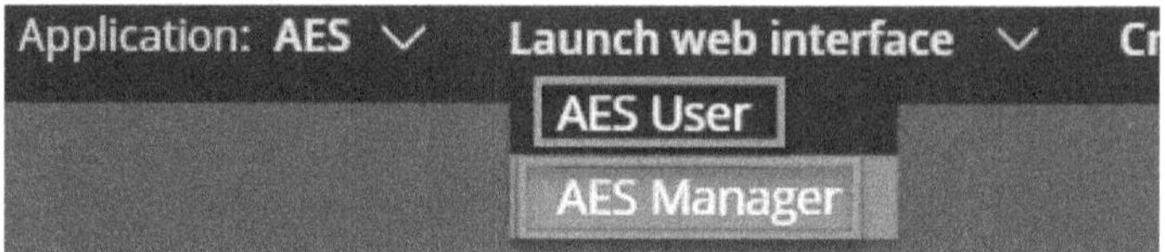

Figure 40: Launching the AES User / AES Manager Portal

You should be able to see the respective portal, like the following:

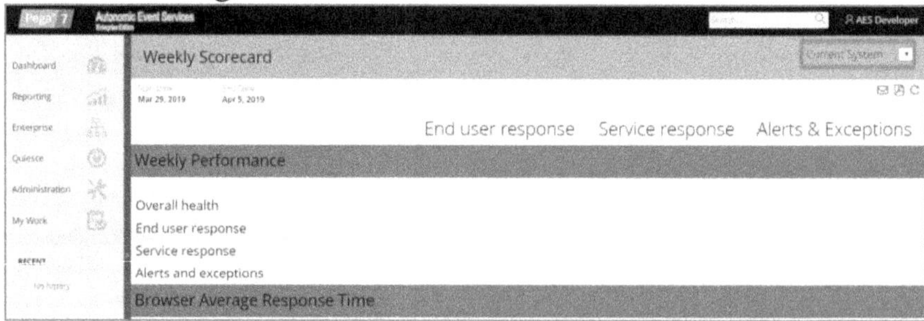

Figure 41: Example of AES Portal

Note that the "Current System" drop-down list does not contain anything. This is because you have not added any monitored system yet!

Configuring the Monitored System

Now that you have installed and tested the AES, you should configure a system for monitoring. The first thing that you need to do is to give the monitored node a name.

Give a New System Name to the Node to be Monitored

Login to the node to be monitored as an administrator, e.g. `administrator@pega.com` with the default password of `install`.

Once you have login, click *Designer Studio > System > Settings > System Name*:

Figure 42: Menu Navigation for Changing System Name

In the form that appears as shown below, enter your new system name in the field: *"New Name"*. In my case, I am renaming it as "MyVM2".

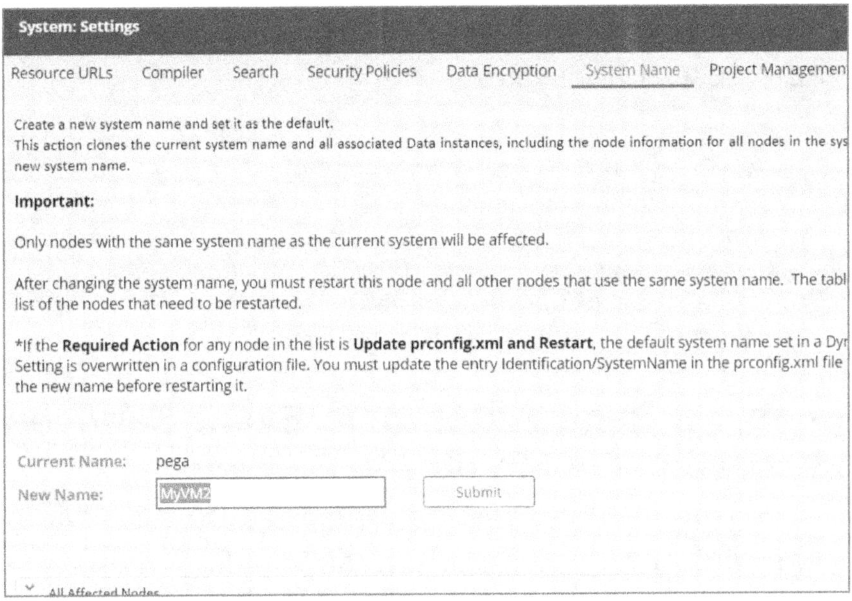

Figure 43: Renaming the System Name

Click the "Submit" button above to save your changes. You will receive the following confirmation:

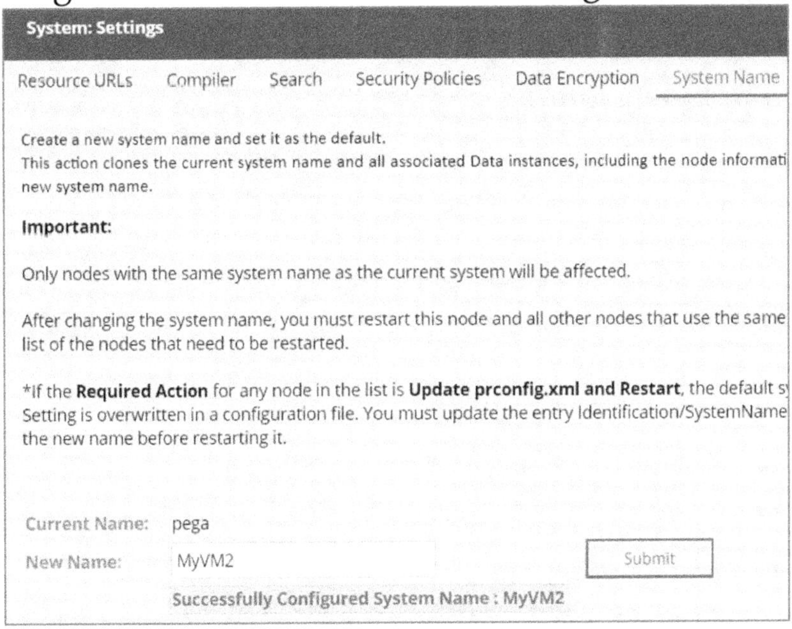

Figure 44: Successfully Configured System Name

Once you have successfully configured the system name, restart the system.

> *If this is a multi-node system, you need to restart all the nodes.*

> *Remember to apply monitored systems hotfixes right after you have configured the system for monitoring with Pega Autonomic Event Services. For applicable hotfixes for your system, always check with Pega Support.*

Enabling Pega Autonomic Event Services Integration On Monitored Systems

Once your system is back online, login to the <u>system to be monitored</u>, as an administrator (e.g. using the `administrator@pega.com` with the default password of `install`).

In the Designer Studio, clicked:
Designer Studio > System > Settings > Predictive Diagnostic Cloud:

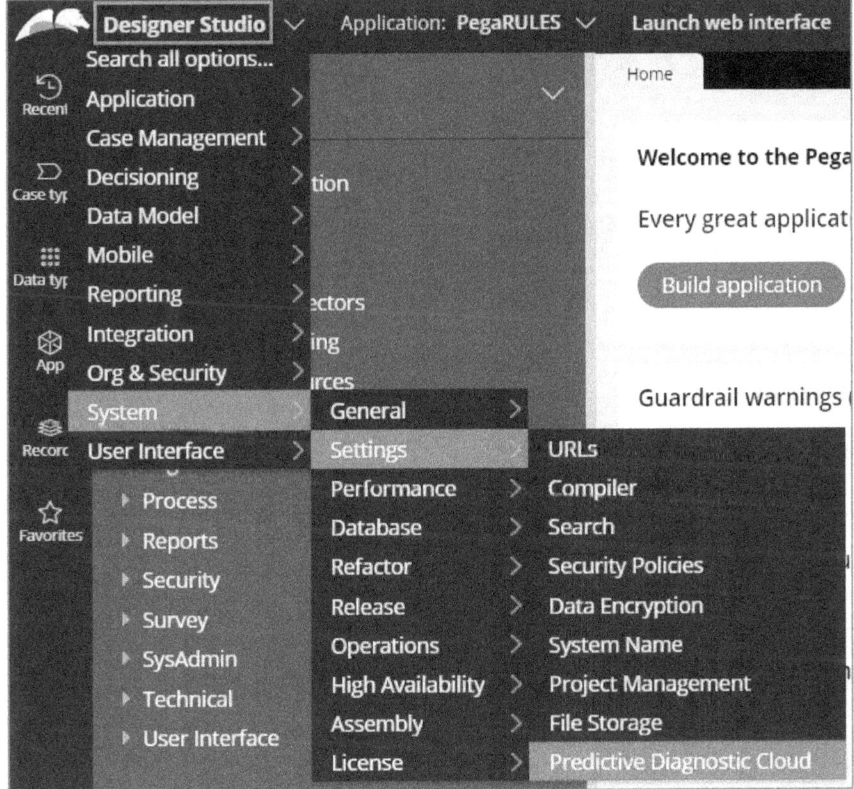

Figure 45: Accessing the Predictive Diagnostic Cloud Settings

In the screen that opens, in the "ENDPOINT SOAP URL" field, enter the endpoint SOAP URL that corresponds to the Pega Autonomic Event Services server's SOAP URL.

In other words, this URL should point to the server that you have installed the AES.

The format is as follows:

http://[server name]:[port number]/prweb/PRSOAPServlet

The following is an example of the setting:

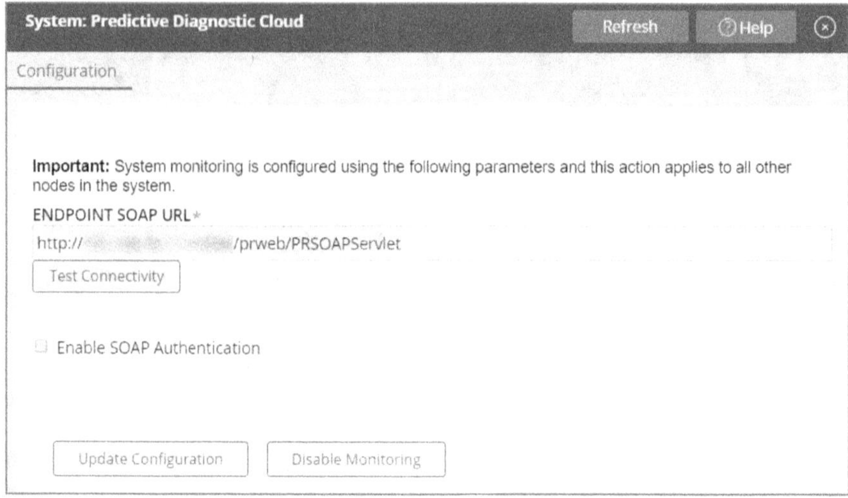

Figure 46: Setting for Predictive Diagnostic Cloud

Ensure that your AES server is up and running before proceeding to the next step.

After that, click on the "Test Connectivity" button, and you should have a success message like the following:

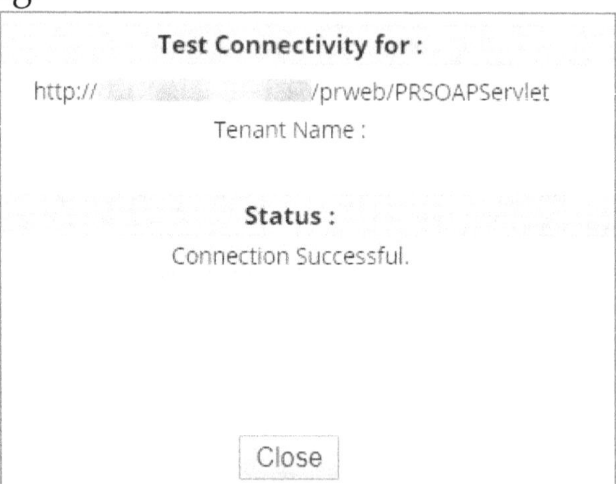

Figure 47: Connection to AES Server Successful

Once your connection is successful, click on the "Update Configuration" button, and you should see the *"Successfully updated Predictive Diagnostic Cloud configuration"* as shown below:

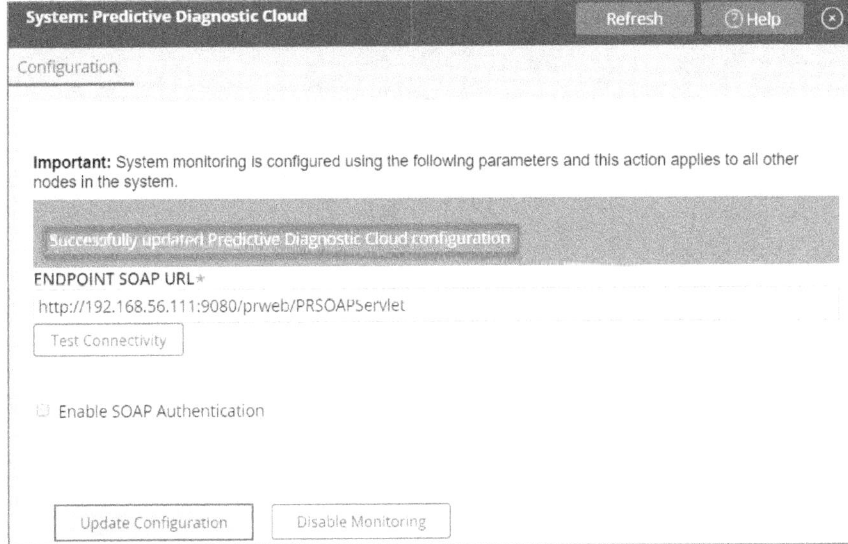

Figure 48: Successfully Updated the Predictive Diagnostic Cloud Configuration

In the installation guide, you were told to use the following format:
<kbd>http://[server name]:[port number]/prweb/PRSOAPServlet</kbd>
However, that does not work.

End-To-End Testing

Now that you have configured both the AES server as well as the monitored system, let's do a final end-to-end testing.

Ensure Monitored System is Registered

Go back to the AES Server, login as `aesmanager` (default password is `password`).

You should notice that under the "Current System", your newly configured monitored system is now shown, in my case, "MyVM2". You can click on the refresh button (the round clockwise circular icon, below the "Current System"), to refresh the data. Of course, there is nothing interesting at this moment of time.

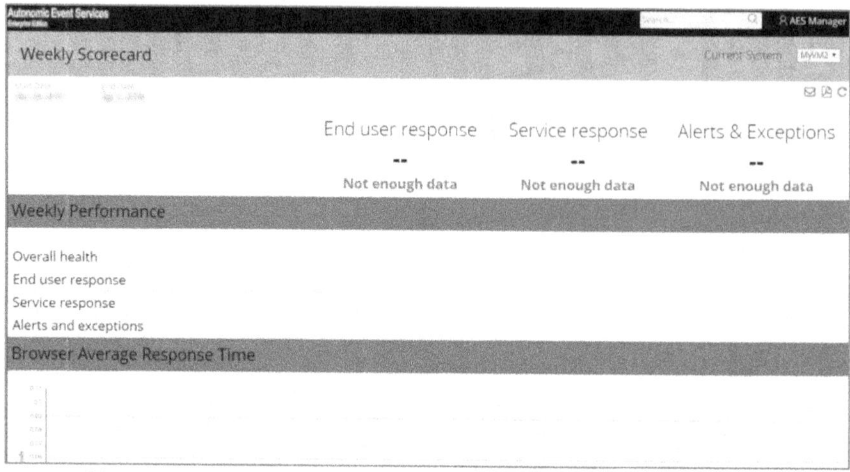

Figure 49: AES Showing the Newly Configured Monitored System

Ensured Monitored System is Fine

The first thing to do, and something that you should do periodically (e.g. every morning), is to ensure that the general health of your monitored system is fine.

To check that, just click on the "Enterprise" button shown below:

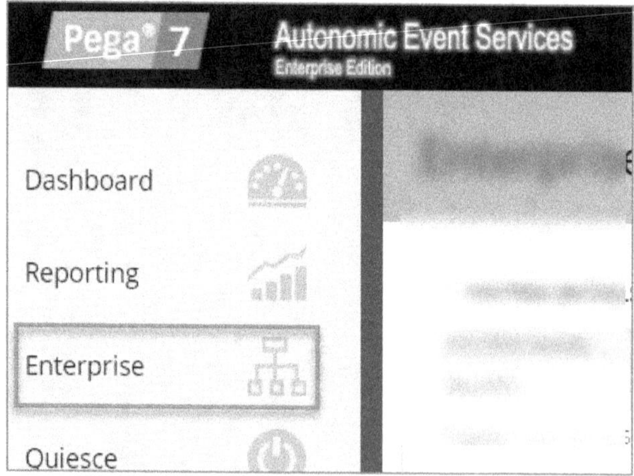

Figure 50: Checking Enterprise Health

You would then be presented with the following:

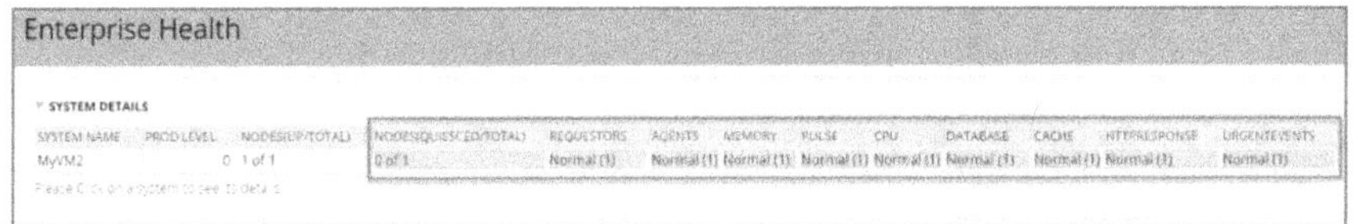

Figure 51: Enterprise Health of All Monitored Systems

The key point is to ensure that you have all the items shown in GREEN.

You can also click on the row, to reveal the "System Details" as shown below.

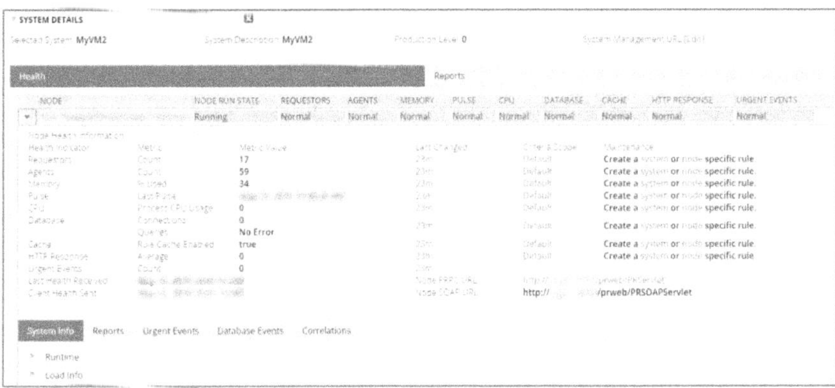

Figure 52: System Details of Selected Node

Conclusion

Pega AES is a very powerful tool, with a very intuitive user interface to help you to monitor all of your systems.

In this ***Debunkum Beaver Pega How-to Guide: Installing and Testing AES***, I had walkthrough how to install and test your AES.

Now, take your new AES for a spin!

Other Books in the Collections

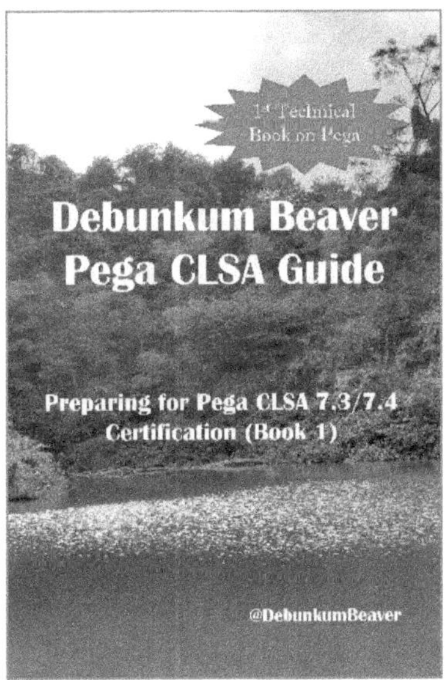

ISBN: 9789811703102
ISBN: 9781796641936

Watch out for more releases at:
URL: https://www.DebunkumBeaver.com
Twitter: https://twitter.com/DebunkumBeaver